100 IDEAS
FOR TRAINEE TEACHERS

CONTINUUM ONE HUNDREDS SERIES

100 IDEAS
FOR TRAINEE
TEACHERS

Angella Cooze

continuum
LONDON • NEW YORK

Continuum International Publishing Group

The Tower Building   80 Maiden Lane
11 York Road   Suite 704
London   New York
SE1 7NX   NY 10038

www.continuumbooks.com

© Angella Cooze 2006

All rights reserved. No part of this publication may be reproduced or transmitted in any form or by any means, electronic or mechanical, including photocopying, recording, or any information storage or retrieval system, without prior permission in writing from the publishers.

Angella Cooze has asserted her right under the Copyright, Designs and Patents Act, 1988, to be identified as Author of this work.

British Library Cataloguing-in-Publication Data
A catalogue record for this book is available from the
British Library.

ISBN: 0–8264–8653–3 (paperback)

Library of Congress Cataloging-in-Publication Data
A catalog record for this book is available from the
Library of Congress

Typeset by Ben Cracknell Studios
Printed and bound in Great Britain by MPG Books Ltd,
Bodmin, Cornwall

CONTENTS

SECTION 4   Behaviour Management

SECTION 11 Useful Information

Preparing for Your Training

In order to be awarded Qualified Teacher Status, a trainee must show that they have met the various competences outlined in the Standards. These are outcome statements that specify the knowledge, understanding and skills that a trainee must demonstrate by the end of their teacher training. As such, the Standards are often used to shape much of the content of teacher training courses, as well as forming the basis for assessment. It is, therefore, useful to have some understanding of the criteria by which you will be evaluated. The full details are readily available on the TTA website – www.tta.gov.uk – but here is a brief outline for you to consider. In England, the Standards are arranged in three sections. This is slightly different in Wales although the content and competencies, in the main, remain the same.

Knowledge and understanding. While this does mean that you should be secure in your subject knowledge, it doesn't stop there. You need to show, among other things, that you are aware of the relevant National Curriculum requirements, strategies and guidelines; that you can use ICT effectively in your lessons; that you are aware of the skills and concepts your pupils will need to be familiar with at various stages of their school career; that you show awareness of how pupils learn and the factors that may influence or affect this; and that you understand what you can expect of your pupils. The list is not endless but does, perhaps, have a broader remit than some trainees may expect. In England, you will also have to pass the skills tests in numeracy, literacy and ICT.

Professional values and practice. This section of the Standards is derived from the General Teaching Council's Professional Code, and outlines the approach, attitudes and dedication expected. This includes, for example, a commitment to the educational achievement of your pupils; a demonstration of positive attitudes and conduct; an understanding of, and contribution to, the life of the school; an awareness of statutory requirements and responsibilities; an ability to communicate with parents and carers; an understanding of the role of support staff; and reflective evaluation and professional development.

Teaching. This large section is split into three areas: planning, expectations and targets; monitoring and assessment; and teaching and class management. As such, it has the most direct bearing on your day to day teaching of your subject. It includes supporting pupils' various needs; providing resources; setting challenging and meaningful tasks and objectives; evaluating progress using a range of strategies; recording and monitoring progress and attainment; and having high expectations and clear frameworks for behaviour management. This section covers the aspects of your class teaching that will be assessed and you would be wise to familiarize yourself with it.

The Standards are a legal requirement – if they are not met Qualified Teacher Status cannot be awarded. Familiarize yourself with them early on and ensure that you work towards meeting each one. Keep records, plans and documents that might act as evidence of your progress. You have to *show* that you have met each Standard; *knowing* that you have is not always enough.

Towards the end of or during your training, you will be asked to complete the first section of a Career Entry Profile (CEP) in Wales or a Career Entry and Development Profile (CEDP) in England. The remaining sections or points are completed during your induction year. The two differ in organization and format, but have a common purpose. Essentially, they are a booklet or folder-style document that you will work on with the support of your mentor, and which you take with you into your first year of teaching, during which time it will act as a guideline for your induction.

You will be asked to reflect upon your strengths as a teacher and also to identify those areas in which you would like to develop further, along with *how* you aim to improve in those areas. The CEP and CEDP both provide a clear link between your teacher training, your induction year and beyond.

It is important to see the CEP or CEDP as more than simply a paper exercise. With thought and reflection, you really could end up with a clear focus that can provide a blueprint for your training and development during your initial year of teaching and beyond. Try to ensure that you are honest in your evaluation of your teaching – this isn't an exam, but a working set of guidelines for your development. The method is as important as the outcome – discussion with tutors, honest reflection, the setting of goals and so on encourage you to focus on how you see yourself developing as a teacher. Remember that your CEP or CEPD is not a static historical document of your weaknesses, but rather part of your development as a teacher.

Throughout your training it is likely that you will write self-evaluations and action plans for development, and discuss your progress at regular intervals. This process is continued in your CEP or CEDP.

Transition point 1 (CEPD) or Section A (CEP) will be the section that is completed and signed by your tutor at the end of your initial teacher training year. It encourages you to identify your strengths and your development interests and needs in preparation for your induction year. It is valuable to use lesson observations, action plans, self-evaluations, progress reports and so on to help you gain a more complete picture of your progress so far and to identify any development needs. You do not have to write a lengthy essay. You can complete your CEP or CEDP in bullet points, note form or paragraphs, as long as it is clear.

Be sure to recognize your strengths. All too often trainees approach this process with a focus on what they perceive to be their weaknesses. Identify what you do well, as well as those areas that may require further development. Remember too that 'development' does not simply mean identification of those areas you feel less confident about, but rather those areas that you would like to explore further too. Don't make a huge unmanageable list of areas that need further improvement. Be specific and realistic. Generally, you will have agreed key areas with your mentor and tutor. Think carefully about *how* you will go about enhancing the areas you have identified, as your goals should be achievable if they are to be meaningful. Also, you may be expected to show how you have improved in your identified areas for action, or where and why your objectives may have changed during your induction year. You might think that you will need to observe certain types of lesson, read key literature or go on training sessions. In many cases, more money is available to your school during the first year of your teaching for you to attend training and development courses than at any other time in your teaching career. Find out what is available and feasible, and make the most of development opportunities.

The demands of a teacher training course include writing and researching assignments as well as teaching and all that it involves. Many of you will not have written assignments of this nature for some time. Some of you may never have written this kind of assignment, or at least not done so since you finished your GCSEs. Remember that you cannot afford to take this part of your course lightly – not only do these assignments give you the opportunity to consider key debates and themes in education, but your successful completion of the course depends upon it. Most assignments will have a very specific remit, perhaps asking you to reflect upon and discuss a particular aspect of your teaching or series of lessons in the context of theory and research.

Be sure that you don't rush your essays. Tempting as it may be to leave them to the very last minute, an all night essay session will not produce the results of which you are most capable, nor will it do your stress levels any good. It is likely that you will need to provide or discuss evidence from your lessons as part of your assignments – you need to be sure that you begin to gather this early, rather than finding out too late that you should have spent the past few weeks collating substantiation.

Check any available marking criteria and read the remit carefully. You will need to know what is expected of you. If you are at all unsure, ask your tutor for clarification. Be sure to make clear links between the findings of research and theory and your own experiences. Remember also that you need to be aware of the expected style and standards of writing. Check rules for referencing quotations and so on. If you are unsure or lacking confidence ask for advice. Many institutions run courses designed to help trainees unused to essay writing develop their skills in this area.

During the first few weeks of your teaching practice, you will observe a variety of lessons. It is quite usual to find yourself observing lessons in a number of subject areas, and highly likely that you will observe lessons that are taught in very different ways. It is important to remember that your role is that of observer, not commentator, assessor or judge. Similarly, fight the urge to participate unless you are invited to do so.

You may be given a proforma that guides your observation, highlighting key areas and focusing your attention on specific features. If not, ensure that your observations are meaningful. Don't just sit passively in a lesson – look at how the teacher is organizing learning.

o What starter tasks are used?
o How many tasks are there and are they differentiated?
o Are they of different types?
o What resources are used?
o Are there any support assistants in the class? What is their role?
o How do the class enter the room and start the lesson?
o How is the register called?
o How are transitions managed?
o How is the noise level controlled?
o How is questioning used?
o How is the room arranged?
o Is there a seating plan?
o How are the class dismissed?
o Are lesson aims made explicit?
o How does the teacher use their voice and body language?
o Who hands out equipment?
o What is the pace of the lesson?
o How are latecomers dealt with?
o How does the teacher monitor the class?

There are, of course, any number of features and aspects that could be commented upon in any lesson. The above may give you some pointers. You might choose to focus your attention on, say, four key features and observe how different teachers manage these particular aspects. You might adopt a more flexible approach and note the features that present themselves in each lesson. Again, try not to observe passively. Think about why a teacher might do something in a particular way. You are in a privileged position and much can be learned during your observational period if you take the opportunity presented to you.

A feature of successful teaching – during your training and throughout your career – is your ability to evaluate and reflect upon your practice. Teaching is a profession that involves continuous development of skills and knowledge, and during your training this development is concentrated into a fairly intensive time period. Your capacity for self-assessment and reflection can be a mark of your professional commitment to developing and improving your teaching.

During your first few weeks of teaching practice, it is not uncommon to be so relieved that a lesson is over that little reflection or self-evaluation is undertaken. Be sure to set aside time, while the lesson is fresh in your mind, to record how you felt about the lesson; what was successful and why; what was not so successful; what you felt could be improved upon and how, and so forth. Reflection allows you to focus on key aspects of your lesson, as well as the broader picture. Part of this evaluation should include reflecting upon factors other than your own perceptions, such as observations made by teaching staff; pupils' responses; theory, research and guidelines; the Standards, and so on. You may notice patterns emerging that can help you target certain areas of your teaching and identify where you may need to seek advice. Without effective reflection, it can be difficult to focus on improving your practice in anything other than a vague manner. Your evaluation and reflection should inform your practice which will in turn inform your evaluation and reflection and so on.

SELF-ASSESSMENT AND REFLECTION

COPING WITH CRITICISM

During your training, your practice will be evaluated and commented upon throughout. There will undoubtedly be aspects of your teaching that will require development and focus, and others that you find come more easily to you. It is important to try not to compare your progress too closely or harshly with that of other trainees. While the sharing of experiences is a vital part of your training, each trainee progresses in their own way and comparing yourself to others is not always helpful.

One of the key ways in which you will progress will be through reflecting and acting upon advice and observations and, as with many aspects of teaching, it is important that you do not take any suggestions for improvement as a personal slight. Similarly, try not to blame the class, the weather, the topic or anything else. Remember that you are learning, and that process involves some trial and error – nobody expects you to be perfect. React professionally to any suggestions or criticisms – you will often know if something hasn't gone to plan anyway. Ask how you could improve in a particular area or what you could have done differently. Take notes, and if there are several elements that need fine-tuning, maybe decide with your observer which ones you should focus on initially. Remember that your training isn't about you collecting positive observation sheets or comments, but rather about you becoming a good teacher. Sometimes criticism may not feel particularly constructive, but even in these rare cases you are learning how to behave and respond in a professional manner. On a similar note, if you feel that your training or any aspect of it is unmanageable, don't keep it to yourself – ask for help. Don't think of it as a weakness. Shouldering a burden alone can often make it worse. Seek support and work on ways of solving your problem.

Introduction to School

As already outlined, during your teacher training you will be expected to provide evidence of your meeting of the Standards. It is a good idea to become practised in carefuly organized filing and record keeping. Nothing can be quite as frustrating as searching for that piece of paper that you need among a heap of others – particularly when somebody is waiting for it. Thorough organization, as well as being of huge practical benefit, can document all aspects of your teaching.

Stock up on lever arch files, dividers and poly pockets prior to starting your course. Teacher training is likely to be very paper oriented. Get into the habit of filing *everything*. Keep separate files organized into workable categories – lesson plans and resources could be filed together, or you could file class by class, for example. Keep any school policies or documents together. File lesson observation records together in date or class order, perhaps along with any self-evaluation undertaken as a result. If you are involved in any extra-curricular activities, keep records. Maintain up-to-date records of pupils' marks, perhaps with anonymous samples. Keep level and grade descriptors, as well as mark schemes and any exam syllabuses close to hand. File the agendas and minutes of any meetings you attend.

Ideally, your files should be ready to be examined at any point. An organizational task such as this is really best undertaken from the very start of your training. Filing two days' worth of plans, observations, resources and so on is manageable. Sorting through half a term's worth is no fun at all.

Beginning your first teaching placement can be very stressful, and it is advisable to do as much homework as you can before your first day. This doesn't mean collecting horror stories and apocryphal tales of doom, but instead gathering practical information that will make your initiation into school life that bit easier.

○ Get hold of a school prospectus (you may be given a copy) and check out its website. While these may be a little narrow in perspective, they will give you a clear feel for the place.

○ If possible, make a dummy run of your journey to school. Try to make your trip using the mode of transport you will ordinarily use and, preferably, at the beginning or close of the school day – journey times can stretch at these peak times.

○ Find out how the school day is structured. Most importantly, what time do you need to arrive? When does the school day finish?

○ During the first couple of days of your placement, get hold of a copy of a map or room plan of the school. You will need to know the location of a significant number of rooms and be able to journey from one to the other swiftly. This can be quite daunting in a large school. Believe it or not, pupils may not *always* provide you with accurate directions!

○ Similarly, learn the names of members of staff. Most will come over time, but you should make an effort to learn key names. Asking a pupil to deliver a message to 'that tall woman, dark hair, you know, bit of a funny walk' is not professional.

GETTING YOUR BEARINGS

During your teaching practice you will usually be expected to act as a member of staff. This means that even if you have only one lesson during a particular day, you will be expected to remain in school until the end of the school day – which may include after school meetings. It is important to remember that your internal clock may have to undergo a gear shift or two – no more midweek lie-ins or late nights out. If you tend to be a late riser, it can be useful to get ready for your school placement by retraining your body clock for the fortnight before your placement.

On a more general note, be sure that you familiarize yourself quickly with the school day. Be sure that you know when you should arrive – not when your first lesson starts but when you should be in school. Important messages and news are often given out at the start of the day and tardiness doesn't go down well. Don't rush out of the door cheering when the bell rings at the end of the day. Act professionally. This can be a good time to gather materials, prepare photocopying, meet with your mentor or other staff members and so on. Know when lunch and break times occur. It is not unknown for pupils to 'test' a trainee by maintaining that lunch has in fact started and that your bell is broken. Similarly, familiarize yourself with lesson times. By feeling confident in your understanding of the school day you will appear, feel and function as a far more organized, controlled and professional person.

Schools, much like many workplaces, are varied and sometimes delicate places that run to a set of unspoken rules that are sometimes only made apparent once breached. As a trainee, you are in quite a peculiar position – a guest, yet also a working member of the staff team. Until you are familiar with the rules, expectations and hidden code of the staffroom, err on the side of caution.

No matter how proud you may be of your septum piercing, neck tattoo or toned midriff, they will generally be unwelcome in school. On your first day, opt for quite formal and smart clothes – think interview rather than ambassador's ball. Once you are more familiar with your school and the way things are done there, you may be able to relax your dress code *a little* by using the appearance of the staff as a guideline. This doesn't mean that if one teacher wears shorts all year that it is okay for you to do the same. It is still advisable to be a little conservative. You are being assessed and judged throughout your time there and, for good or for bad, this is not the time or place to be proudly asserting your original take on fashion. Flesh-baring is, understandably, not a good idea. Ensure that you are smart, clean and covered. While this may seem difficult or unreasonable to some, it makes sense in school – pupils, staff and parents *will* judge you by appearance – and allows you to keep your more expressive side for after school hours.

DAY-TO-DAY PROCEDURES

Ensure that you are familiar with day-to-day procedures, such as booking ICT suites, when and how to send classes to the library or where to get coloured paper. You will appear and feel far more self-sufficient and professional. Similarly, ensure that you know who you need to approach for various matters and where they can be found.

Find out what equipment is available to you, where it is kept, how you book it and who you call upon if it goes wrong. This helps your planning and also enables you to be a little more self-sufficient. Locate the resource area for your department and find out what is available to you, as well as any booking procedures. Be sure to offer your resources to your department – they will be gratefully received. Photocopying can be a surprisingly contentious issue in schools. Don't use up your department's allocation in the first week – never a popular move. Find out where and how photocopying is done and if there is a specific allocation.

Find out what systems are in place for pastoral, academic and other issues and use them accordingly. This can cover everything from booking a day off for an interview to reporting misbehaviour to booking a minibus to locating a mop. Be sure that you identify the chain of command and responsibility, and use it appropriately. You do not want to waste someone's time by asking them to deal with an issue which is not part of their remit, nor do you want to stand on anyone's toes. Knowing who you should turn to also enables you to work more efficiently.

During your teaching practice you will generally be expected to take part in the same school day as other teachers. This is likely to include meetings, parents' evenings and other post-school obligations. The meetings you may attend could be departmental, pastoral, whole-school and so on. It is important that, if you are expected to attend, you turn up. This is part of your professional role and training. If you know you will not be able to make a meeting – for good reason – you must inform your mentor or whoever is responsible for minuting the meeting. If you are unsure as to whether you are expected to be present at meetings, find out – don't simply assume that you will not.

If you are expected to turn up, confirm your role. Generally, certainly in the initial stages of your teaching practice, you will be observing rather than participating. In some meetings – say a pastoral meeting where form issues are discussed or a departmental meeting where teaching matters that directly involve you are talked about – you may be invited to contribute. Ensure that you are prepared and be punctual. Check the agenda and venue and bring any relevant documentation with you. Be aware of protocol for asking questions, raising points, offering information and so on. Take notes of any decisions or information that will be of use. During some meetings, matters of a confidential nature may be discussed. Be sure to act with discretion and professionalism.

Space is at a premium in many schools and people can become, understandably, quite proprietary. Be sure that you respect that you are in a professional environment and sharing space with other staff members.

○ Staffroom – the staffroom is often a haven away from the demands of the classroom and corridors and should be respected as such. It is sometimes organized by invisible rules that may seem arbitrary but help secure the harmonious sharing of a sometimes cramped space. Find out if there are any seating areas that you should avoid, or use. These may be unofficially allocated, but such allocations should be observed nonetheless. While a nice sing-along with your guitar or a water fight may seem to be an excellent way to unwind during a free lesson, others may be trying to work or have some quiet time. Similarly, at least initially, check your language and humour. Staffrooms are populated by a variety of personality types and sarcasm, ribald humour and over-familiarity are not always appreciated by all. Also, be discreet. You are in a professional environment and salacious gossip or moaning about pupils or staff doesn't always go down well. Refreshments can also be a precious commodity in school. Find out what the arrangements and facilities are for tea, coffee and snacks, and provide for yourself accordingly.

○ Classrooms – you will probably teach in a number of rooms and should ensure that they are in a fit state when you leave them. Clear away any resources and litter, and return tables, chairs and equipment to where they were when you arrived. This needs to be done as quickly and efficiently as possible as often a class and their teacher will be waiting outside to start their lesson. You should not keep pupils and staff waiting outside nor should you leave your mess for anyone else to clear up. If you are fortunate enough to have a main teaching room, keep it clutter free and well managed.

The phrase 'school rules' is a little old-fashioned, perhaps. Many schools don't have rules as such, but rather guidelines, codes, expectations, and so on. Nonetheless, schools are communities and, as such, are organized according to systems of explicit expectation. As a trainee, you will be expected to be familiar with school policy on a range of issues. You may be presented with a staff handbook that outlines relevant policy for you, but this is not always the case. As already discussed, preparing yourself for school by establishing a working familiarity with key policies, procedures or 'rules' can really give you a head start confidence wise. As a starting point, find out what you can about those areas most likely to affect you directly. The following may provide a base from which to start.

○ School uniform – what are pupils expected to wear? What are the rules regarding jewellery, shoes and so on? Is there a different uniform for sixth form, for example? What are the procedures if uniform is not worn? Is it your responsibility to deal with it?

○ Lunch and break time procedures – are pupils allowed into school? If so, where?

○ Fire drills – where are pupils to assemble? Do you register your teaching group or registration form?

○ Permission to leave class – for what reasons are pupils allowed to leave your classroom during lesson time? Are slips or passes required?

○ Punctuality and preparation – are there set sanctions/procedures in place for lateness or lack of equipment?

SCHOOL RULES, POLICIES AND PROCEDURES

THE CURRICULUM: A QUICK GUIDE

The National Curriculum is the framework that shapes teaching and learning in schools. Contentious since its introduction, the National Curriculum raises many important questions about the nature of education and the role of the state. The purpose of this idea, however, is not to debate but rather to point out key features.

The National Curriculum is a statutory framework within which schools timetable, organize and deliver teaching and learning. It is comprised of English, mathematics, science, design and technology, information technology, history, geography, music, art, physical education, modern foreign languages and (in England at Key Stage 4) citizenship, which must be taught to all pupils in state schools from the ages of 5–16. Provision must also be made for religious education, sex education and careers education. As well as specifying what subjects must be taught, the National Curriculum also sets out the knowledge and skills that should be taught in each subject. The National Curriculum is arranged in four Key Stages, with programmes of study outlining what should be taught at each Key Stage. Each subject also has attainment targets, which set out the knowledge, skills and understanding pupils should achieve by the end of each Key Stage. These attainment targets include eight level descriptors, which indicate the range and types of pupil performance that may be expected at each level. At the end of each Key Stage, pupils in England will take national tests in core subjects.

As a trainee teacher, you will, of course, have to teach according to the National Curriculum. This isn't quite as daunting as it sounds – departmental schemes of work will be based on its specifications – and you needn't fear losing your individual approach, as while the National Curriculum outlines *what* is to be taught, it doesn't specify *how* it is to be taught.

The Lesson

The Lesson

PLANNING AND PREPARATION

The endless preparation and detailed planning that is an unavoidable feature of teaching practice can feel like a weighty burden on an already heavy load. Sometimes, in the face of other more pressing concerns, such as class management or resource preparation, the lesson plan can be the first thing to be sacrificed, becoming a brief, hastily scribbled list of tasks rather than a meaningful guide to the aims of a lesson. This is a real shame, as detailed planning *does* result in more productive teaching and learning – time consuming though it is.

The reasons for this are manifold, but the most obvious perhaps are that, prior to your lesson, successful planning helps you to understand *how* you are going to fulfil your aims for the lesson, and, during the lesson, provides you with a clear structure and focus (a life-raft even at times!). A common feature of planning in the earlier stages of teaching practice is a tendency for plans to be task-led (that is, *what* the pupils will do) rather than aim-led (*why* they will do it). Your planning focus should be on what your pupils will have *learned* rather than the tasks they will be given in the process. Start planning from the aim downwards. That is, establish the skills, knowledge, understanding and so on you wish your pupils to have obtained by the end of your lesson and then work out *how* you can facilitate this through your tasks and resources.

Having established what your learning objectives are going to be for a given lesson, the next stage is working out how they are going to be achieved. It is at this stage that task setting and resources become the focus, but always as a means to achieving your aims rather than simply devising a timed list of activities. Two factors need to be taken into account when devising your plan. These are:

○ The profile of the class – your tasks should be pitched so as to ensure that all pupils in your class will be able to attempt *and* understand them. It is vital, particularly in the early days of teaching, that you use all available data, along with the knowledge and experience of the class teacher, so as to ensure that your lessons are appropriate and well pitched. Depending on the make-up of your class, some tasks will be more easily accessed by some pupils and some may provide more detailed or complex responses, but you should have baseline concepts and skills that are accessible to all. That is, your main learning objective should be achievable by the whole class. This ensures that your learning objectives are met by all pupils and that each pupil has a valid learning experience in your lessons. Even in sets, there will be a range of ability as well as differing attitudes and preferred styles of learning, and so it is important to ensure that you provide extension and support opportunities in your planning, not simply on an ad hoc basis during the lesson itself.

○ Methods and activities – successful lessons will usually incorporate a variety of activities so as to engage different types of learner.

DEVISING A LESSON PLAN

TASK SETTING

Your tasks are the vehicle by which your pupils arrive at their learning destination. Terrible metaphors aside, a task is not an end in itself, but rather a way of communicating or developing skills, knowledge and understanding. A variety of well-pitched, appropriate, purposeful and well-organized tasks should be your aim for every lesson.

Tasks are often used as stages leading to the achievement of an overall aim. Think backwards from your key learning objective(s) for the lesson. Once you have established where you want to go, you need to devise tasks that will get you there.

While it may sometimes be unavoidable, it is a good general rule to avoid over-reliance on long individual tasks – especially with younger pupils or when introducing a topic or skill. Short, snappy tasks – particularly as starter tasks – can engage pupils. Build up confidence and knowledge (and maintain focus) through staged tasks. Each task should have a discrete aim which contributes to the overall learning objective. If possible and appropriate (keeping an eye on pace), encourage feedback or sharing of responses at the end of each task and introduce the next as growing out of the knowledge gained during that just completed. This can be organized in the way best suited to your class, but it helps pupils to see the point behind what they are doing; to see that it is leading somewhere. Process can be as valuable as end product.

In order to reach as many of your pupils as possible, you should ensure that your tasks do not follow the same format nor rely on the same skills for success. Appeal to as many different types of learner as you can. Pupils often learn best when they apply their knowledge practically, so try to introduce 'doing' or problem-solving tasks into your lessons. Some pupils respond variously to visual or aural stimulus; some learn best through talk; some work best as part of a group; others work best alone. The combinations are endless, but you should try to include a sufficient variety of tasks and groups to appeal to your pupils as learners. This is not to suggest that you cram each lesson to the brim with variety. It is a lesson, after all, and not a variety show. Some types of tasks will be more suited to some lessons and classes than others and variety for variety's sake benefits no one really.

In all classes there will be a range of ability. In some classes that range will be significant. Some pupils may find certain aspects of your subject difficult and some will struggle with the subject per se. Use your developing knowledge of the class to provide support and extension tasks as needed. Liaise with the class teacher and learning support assistants – make the most of their experience.

As you become more familiar with curriculum demands and the needs of your pupils, you will learn how best to support and extend their learning.

TASK SETTING AND THE NEEDS OF YOUR PUPILS

LESSON RESOURCES

Just as your tasks are the means to meeting your learning objectives, so are your resources the means through which your tasks are presented. Resources can come from any number of sources – books, newspaper articles, ready-made books or sheets, dedicated websites. Initially, you may find that you tend towards using resources that have been devised with or by others, largely because of lack of confidence. The proliferation of websites dedicated to classroom resources is both a blessing and a curse. There is often no quality control; they may pertain to the specifics of a very different curriculum and year group or ability range; they will certainly not pertain to the specifics of your class; there are so very many to wade through that sifting through can be as time consuming as starting from scratch; pupils may see that tell-tale web address at the bottom of the page and react a little dismissively. Web resources, much like any shared resources, can be beneficial, particularly in the early days of your teaching. You can get ideas that can be adapted to suit the needs of your class and some tasks and suggestions have been tried, tested and found resoundingly successful. The key is to remember that your resources should be pitched to your class rather than follow an 'off the peg one size fits all' approach. It is also important to remember that an eye-catching, well-presented resource is only really commendable if it facilitates learning – colourful illustrations or bouncing letters don't count for anything, other than as a minor distraction. The content should be there.

Purpose and audience – your first consideration should, of course, be your aims for the lesson and the needs of your pupils. For example, a treasure hunt style resource may be appropriate to teach investigatory skills to your Year 8 class, but may be inappropriate for Year 11.

○ Clarity – no matter what form your resources may take, it is important that they are clear and focused. Try not to overfill worksheets or presentations with too much clutter. Key information and questions need to be clear and highlighted. Too much information at once can confuse many pupils and dilute focus.

○ Structure – as well as being clear, your resources should have a purposeful structure. Pupils should be able to work through a resource (or set of resources) and have developed or enhanced a skill, understanding or knowledge by its end. They should, if appropriate, be staged, so that tasks build upon each other.

○ Variety – try to use a number of types of resource. The repeated use of a rigid formula worksheet can be uninspiring for both you and your pupils. Also, certain tasks simply work better in particular formats. Appeal to the different pupils in your class – use audio and visual resources; utilize your ICT skills inventively; devise problem-solving games. Be creative!

USING RESOURCES EFFECTIVELY – SOME TIPS

MORE TIPS ON RESOURCES

○ Sharing and adapting – having focused on the importance of developing a body of specific resources, there remains a place for shared, ready-made and adapted resources. While devising resources really does help focus your attention on your task setting, there is, as they say, no need to reinvent the wheel every single time. Teachers you work with may have tried and tested resources that may be perfect for your lesson. These can also act as models, to an extent, for your own resources. Just be sure to check that the resource is suitable for your particular class and aims.

○ Differentiation – as mentioned previously, even in set classes ability may differ considerably. Use your knowledge of the pupils to ensure that your resources are accessible to all. Be sensitive – don't hand out sheets and then give Sara one which is clearly different from the others. Remember too, that differentiation doesn't simply mean 'easier', but rather ensuring that all of your pupils can be involved in and challenged by your tasks. This may mean increasing font size; using sheets of different colours; providing extension tasks to stretch the most able; adding more scaffolding and support – you will know the needs of your pupils and your resources should reflect this.

○ Worksheet dependency – it is worth remembering that 'resource' is not another name for 'worksheet'. Over-dependency on the worksheet can be problematic and limiting. Remember that, as outlined in Idea 23, your resources should be varied and engaging. Remember also that your resources for a given lesson may include things such as felt pens, sugar paper, videos and so on. If these things are not prepared and ready, your lesson can quickly disintegrate.

You may find yourself surprised at just how wide the range of ability can be in a classroom. Sometimes, particularly when teaching younger pupils, it is easy to forget that pupils will often lack skills that may seem rudimentary to you. You have the rather daunting job of making your subject accessible and engaging for your pupils, while stretching and developing their knowledge, skills and understanding.

Pitching lessons to the right level is a skill that really does develop with time and experience. Every aspect of teaching informs another – for example, ignoring assessment data can lead to inappropriately pitched lessons, which can in turn impact on class management.

Gather as much information about your class as you can. Look at levels and grades of work submitted. What is the range? Are there any patterns? Speak to the usual class teacher about what they have found works best with a particular class and use your observation time wisely – make notes.

Look at the mark scheme and grade/level criteria for the aspect of your subject that you will be teaching. While this should not be used as the basis for a lesson plan, it *can* provide information regarding the spread and depth of skills at a particular range of levels or grades, and, importantly, how pupils can move up the through the levels.

THE IMPORTANCE OF PITCHING
TO THE RIGHT ABILITY

You will fine-tune your pitching with experience, but the following may help you pitch your lessons in such a way as to facilitate learning, rather than confuse or turn off your pupils.

o Build up to skill or knowledge acquisition through stepped tasks. That is, lead up to your lesson objective through staged tasks that develop and build upon the previous task. The number of steps and the gradient will differ from class to class, but the principle remains the same. Again, mark schemes can be useful here, as your tasks can be pitched so as to enable pupils to progress through the mark scheme by which they will be assessed.

o Your pupils will often be the first to let you know if tasks are pitched accurately. Finishing tasks in very little time, boredom and frustration, and little detail in responses are just some of the indicators that your lesson might not be reaching its audience. Circulate, and monitor understanding. If necessary, stop and explain again, or introduce another stage if you feel confident enough. Remember that a quiet class is not necessarily an indication of your prowess or their understanding.

o Assessment should be used to inform your task setting and pitching. Assessment – formal and informal – should be used to assess not only pupils' learning, but also your own teaching. You should note any patterns, or areas in which you will need to provide extra support or extension.

Pupils – as do all people – learn in different ways. While some pupils may respond well to verbal instructions, others may need visual or kinaesthetic stimuli. Considerable research has been done on the various learning styles and types of intelligence, and they have been categorized in a number of ways. The following is a brief outline using terms that may be of most use in the classroom.

Learning styles can be roughly divided into three categories. Most people do not fit neatly into a single category, but rather have dominant tendencies.

○ Visual learners – these types of learner learn through seeing. They tend to respond well to diagrams, illustrations, flip charts.
○ Auditory learners – these types of leaner learn through listening. They respond well to discussion, lectures.
○ Kinaesthetic learners – these types of learner learn through doing. They prefer to practise skills, rather than read or hear about them.

As part of an effective lesson, you should provide opportunities for learning that appeal to different learning styles. No one teaching style will suit all pupils. Be sure that you give your pupils the opportunity to learn in the way that best suits them. Provide a variety of tasks that will appeal to each learning style and motivate each pupil. Also bear in mind that tasks rather than tools are the best way to provide a variety of meaningful learning opportunities.

LEARNING STYLES

Learning styles are not concrete and distinct, but by identifying a pupil's preferred learning style you can help them get the most out of your lessons. The following suggestions may provide a basis for you to establish what kind of learning a pupil tends towards, but the list is not exhaustive.

○ Visual learners – remember what they see rather than what they hear, and describe things in visual images. They are often well-organized and presentation matters to them. They may tend to doodle and decorate. Written instructions are often easier for them to follow than verbal. They are often strong readers. They may, for example, respond to colour-coded board displays.

○ Auditory learners – sometimes talk or read to themselves. They enjoy reading aloud or listening to stories, may enjoy discussion and are often articulate. They can often tell a story better than they can write it. They may need to spell a word out loud in order to spell correctly. They may, for example, respond to discussing what is written on the board.

○ Kinaesthetic learners – may find sitting still difficult. They may stand close to people and use touch or movement to get attention or illustrate a point. Their handwriting may be untidy. They enjoy games and activity and may get bored easily. They may prefer role-play and practical application of skills. They may, for example, respond to coming up to the board and highlighting key features.

IDENTIFY DIFFERENT LEARNING STYLES

Giving clear instructions and explaining tasks or information effectively are all important parts of a successful lesson. As with many aspects of teaching, to be effective they need to be considered and purposeful.

Your instructions need to be clear and easily understood. Instructions that have multiple parts are confusing and can lead to problems. Remember what it can be like if you ask for directions in a strange place – after three or so instructions it all becomes rather vague and you forget what was said first. Limit instructions to around three clear, key directives at a time. If possible and appropriate, display these instructions to the class on the board or IWB as a reference point. Once these instructions have been followed, more can be given, perhaps following some monitoring of understanding and progress. Be sure to give instructions in a clear voice. There must be quiet and pupils need to be facing you. You can check understanding by asking a pupil to confirm what it is the class now have to do. Give pupils some sense of timing in which the instructions are to be carried out and, where appropriate, a sense of continuity and purpose.

Similarly, when you are explaining a concept or task pupils need to be quiet and you need to be the focus of the room. Again, in the main, lengthy lecture style exposition is not usually the best method. Your explanations need to be purposeful and well pitched. Key ideas, information and so on can be illustrated and reinforced on the board, worksheets or IWB. You can check understanding by way of well-placed questions or by breaking off to set a task, for example.

INSTRUCTING AND EXPLAINING

Effective questioning really is invaluable as a teaching and learning tool. The well-placed question can encourage pupils to, among many other things, engage with knowledge, reflect upon information, consolidate learning, apply skills or understanding in a new context and learn from each other.

There are several different types of question that may be used for different learning purposes. For example: recalling previously learned data or definitions; applying knowledge or skills to new situations or contexts; analysing the relationships between different pieces or areas of knowledge; evaluating one piece of information in the light of knowledge or skills gained. As a teacher, your questions might be used to evaluate understanding; sum up a lesson or task; encourage problem solving and reflection or present possibilities. Alongside the reasons behind and outcomes of questioning, there are also different types of question. The clearest distinction is between open and closed questions. An open question has many potential answers ('What adjectives could you use here?'), while a closed question has a limited number of correct responses (What is an adjective?). The majority of classroom questions tend to be low-level. That is, asking pupils to use skills such as recollection and comprehension rather than higher-level skills such as analysis and evaluation. This can be rather limiting, even though these types of question have a valuable place in the classroom. It is important to consider the needs of your pupils and the purpose of your questioning, and to use different types of question as appropriate, perhaps building up to more complex high-level questions once basics have been established. Is the purpose of your questioning to encourage recall and consolidate knowledge? Is it aimed at extension and utilization of skills?

While some questions will emerge naturally through the course of the lesson, key questions should be prepared beforehand. Be sure that you phrase your questions clearly – pupils cannot be expected to respond if they are unsure what is being asked of them. Allow pupils a little time to consider the question – particularly if it requires them to exercise higher-level skills – before expecting a response or rephrasing. Praise and encourage clarification or extension where needed. Whenever appropriate try to elicit responses from different pupils – avoid the 'same hands up' syndrome.

If you are training in a school in England, you are likely to participate in some way in the delivery of the curriculum for citizenship. Citizenship has been a statutory subject in secondary schools in England since 2002 and is also part of the ACCAC guidelines for schools in Wales. As such, you would be wise to check out its Programme of Study (PoS) and Attainment Target.

Citizenship may be taught in a number of different ways. Alongside discrete lessons, many of the principles, and knowledge and understanding outlined in its PoS can be taught as part of other subject lessons. Also, a feature of an effective citizenship programme is pupil participation. That is, giving pupils the opportunity to develop their skills and understanding in a hands on way through their involvement in mock elections; projects within the local community; charity committee meetings and so on.

Three key and connected elements to education for citizenship are:

○ Social and moral responsibility – pupils learn about and develop an understanding of the importance of responsible behaviour and attitudes in and out of the school environment. They develop an understanding of citizens' rights and responsibilities, and how their behaviour and attitudes can contribute to or diminish communities.

○ Community involvement – pupils become aware of and involved in the life of their communities: local, national and global. This may include partaking in community service or projects.

○ Political literacy – developing an understanding of how our democracy works – on a local and national level – and the part individuals can play in the political process. Pupils become aware of forms of government, how public services and legal systems work and how change takes place in society.

MOTIVATING THE DISENGAGED USING ICT AND SHORT, SHARP LESSONS

The debates continue to rage as to the extent, nature, cause, cure and, indeed, even the actual existence of disengaged pupils. Some pupils seem detached from the learning process from time to time, others seem to be wholly disinterested. There may be no hard and fast answers or reasons for this, and it has to be noted that factors beyond the classroom are generally out of our control. Nonetheless, some strategies seem to help. Remember that a quiet class is not the same thing as an engaged class. Many of the suggestions below may be elements of a successful lesson per se, rather than aimed specifically at the disengaged.

o ICT – the effective and guided use of ICT in the classroom seems to have a marked effect on many pupils' attitude to tasks. Where possible and appropriate, try to include ICT as a meaningful part of your lessons. As well as using ICT to present aspects of your lesson to the class, give pupils the opportunity to use ICT themselves.

o Short and sharp – organizing lessons as a series of short, timed tasks is effective in maintaining focus. Where possible, build up to the overall aim of your lesson through timed, directed activities which last for no more than ten minutes. Also, start lessons as soon as pupils enter the classroom. Have lesson starter sheets ready or have a short exercise written on the board before pupils arrive. Remind pupils of the aims of individual tasks and of the overall lesson. Pupils respond well when given the opportunity to understand why they are doing something.

o The positive environment – many pupils respond positively to an encouraging learning environment. Be sure to make tasks achievable, though engaging, and to encourage and reward good work and behaviour. Ensure that your pupils can see short- and longer-term benefits of cooperation and progression. Maintain firm classroom discipline, while also showing sensitivity to a pupil's point of view. Pupils like to feel that they are listened to and that your decisions are reasonable and consistent rather than emotional. Show your own enthusiasm and commitment – this has consistently been shown to be a huge motivating factor.

o Five – it has been found that many pupils respond to the organization of lessons around the number 'five'. This can include, for example, the five-part lesson; being asked to list five facts about a given topic; having five-minute tasks as a part of lessons; five-paragraph plans; five questions and so on. While this sounds quasi-mystical, it is a surprisingly effective organizing principle. Perhaps five is a number which allows for a certain degree of engagement without being daunting and off-putting.

o Seating plans – many schools have whole school or department wide seating plans in place. These may be boy–girl, or organized according to other principles. If there is no such policy or practice it may be useful to adopt your own. This can help to dissipate the tendency some pupils have to perform for their friends.

MOTIVATING THE DISENGAGED
USING THE ENVIRONMENT

Behaviour Management

CLASSROOM MANAGEMENT

Class management – often reduced to control and discipline – is a real worry for many trainees often exacerbated by urban myths and media scaremongering about the dreadful and dangerous places that classrooms have become. While there *are* instances where pupils' behaviour is totally unmanageable or downright dangerous, these are pretty rare and, in the main, the vast majority of class management issues with which you will be dealing will be low level. It should also be some comfort that, while there is no golden set of rules that will forever banish misbehaviour in your lessons, there are certain strategies and routines that can go some way to helping your lessons run smoothly. As a trainee, you are in a rather peculiar position. Much class management, after all, is borne from the relationships developed between a class and its teacher, and within the class itself. These may have been built over years, and you, unfortunately, will not have this kind of relationship. Don't be too disheartened if you do not establish the rapport with a class or pupil that their usual teacher enjoys. It will come. You may also find that, in time, you develop very different working relationships with various classes.

In general, your first meeting with a class can really set the tone for future lessons. This doesn't mean that a bad initial lesson dooms you to an uphill struggle for the remainder of your lessons, but establishing your boundaries and expectations firmly and early can save you much stress and hard slog later on. Interestingly, when asked, most pupils appreciate firm classroom control and feel most comfortable in lessons where there is sound discipline.

A lesson which is well prepared and delivered is key to effective class management – something that will be discussed in Idea 37. Be sure that your first lesson is well planned; that resources (including spares of any equipment pupils will need, such as pens or pencils) are ready and well prepared; the classroom layout is suited to your needs; and that you are there before your pupils, unless exceptional circumstances arise.

Your control of entrances and exits really can determine your relationship with a class. You are, after all, establishing a working relationship and, as with all introductions, first impressions count.

School protocol regarding entrances and exits may vary due to practical considerations, but as a trainee it can be useful to establish a routine governing how you expect pupils to enter your lesson. This demonstrates your authority and places you in a position of control from the start. You may choose to line your pupils up outside the class; expect them to stand quietly behind desks until asked to sit; require them to get out their equipment and prepare for the lesson, or whatever routine suits your particular situation best, given the practical constraints of school life. What is important is that the routine is determined by *you*. That is, *you* provide the instructions for how each pupil is to enter the class and ready themself for learning – the position of instruction-giver is, after all, one of implicit authority. There needs to be a *clearly* marked sense that the pupils are now starting a lesson, and establishing a simple routine for entrance can provide a physical cue for pupils.

As mentioned above, your entrance routine can vary according to what best suits your situation, but it should include your control or direction of noise and of physical movement and should let pupils know you have high expectations from the start. It is a good rule of thumb, certainly initially, to avoid casual conversation and questions during the start of your lesson. You are setting a tone, and focusing on individual pupils can mean you lose the class.

The manner in which you dismiss your class is similarly important. It should be orderly and therefore it is a good idea to actively control class dismissal. Again, you may organize this in the way best suited to your situation, but it is useful to ensure that equipment is put away; the room is uncluttered and orderly; and that the class is quiet and facing you. It is sometimes hard to organize class dismissal efficiently due to time or task constraints, nonetheless it is important to establish and maintain a routine. This helps you build up an image of yourself as a capable practitioner and lets pupils know

ENTRANCES AND EXITS

what is expected of them. Dismiss your class in groups. This helps you maintain control and also avoids the rush for the door and subsequent squash of bodies. These routines need to be repeated until they become expected and then automatic.

Having controlled pupils' entrance to the classroom, place yourself in a prominent position – usually the front of the class – and instruct pupils to face you, quietly, while you introduce yourself. Initiate interaction – ask a pupil their name and then give them a task to perform, such as handing out books, or opening a window. These sorts of interactions imply your status in the classroom. You are showing, without any confrontation and with self-assurance, that you direct the action in the classroom. It may also be useful in initial lessons to instigate a seating plan. This enables you to learn names – vital in good class management – and also to move potential pockets of trouble.

Pupils will be interested in sizing you up, but avoid both the rambling prologue and answering the personal questions that often crop up. Be brisk and professional in your introduction – you are not on a first date – and, if you feel it will be useful, set out your ground rules and expectations. Many trainees use their first lesson with a class for just this purpose – explaining the rules that will govern the coming lessons, with varying degrees of negotiation with the class, and then displaying them as a poster or in pupils' books. These rules should be in keeping with school policy, as should any sanctions. It is good practice to let pupils know what will be expected of them in advance.

It is often useful to avoid these rules being a lengthy list with clauses and sub-clauses. To be most effective, your expectations and rules should be easily understood and fair. If possible, phrase them positively: 'do' rather than negatively 'don't'. They may vary from class to class, but must include an understanding that talking when you are addressing the class will not be tolerated. The trick is then to ensure that you, as well as your pupils, stick to them consistently.

Your entrance routine will already have acted as an introduction to your expectations of the class. The next stage is, in the initial lessons, to consolidate this and to assert yourself. Almost every trainee will hear the old adage 'Don't smile 'til Christmas', and while a grim, impenetrable and rigidly dictatorial classroom persona may not be advisable and would perhaps strip some of the joy from teaching, it is certainly worth adopting a more firm and serious manner than that which you may employ later. This can feel quite alien initially, almost as if you are playing a role, and to a degree you are. Teaching *does* have an element of performance, supported by props, script and costume.

You will of course, having paid very close attention to the section on dress code, be looking the part, and your time spent in preparation will mean that your 'props' – resources, pens, plans and so on – are ready. During your introductory dealings with your class, you need to establish your position as one of implicit authority. This can be difficult in such a nerve-racking situation and is where elements of performance come in. You should aim to present yourself as confident, purposeful and in charge – even if you feel anything but. The following Ideas include suggestions through which you can establish your authority. They can be adapted to suit your needs and situation.

An understanding of how to best utilize your body language is an important part of looking and feeling confident in the classroom. Used well, a look or (appropriate) gesture can be much more effective than words. Unfortunately, your body language also gives away a lot of clues. If you appear hunched and fidgety, pupils will read your insecurity, no matter what you say. Similarly, an aggressive stance can suggest that you are expecting confrontation, while appearing too relaxed can indicate indifference. Using body language to appear confident, enthusiastic and in control, without seeming dominating, can seem a quite precarious balancing act. The following tips can help you appear more at ease.

○ Tempting as it may be sometimes, sitting down while delivering your lesson may be comfy, but it is not effective. Whether presenting to the whole class, monitoring pupils' work or observing responses, you will generally be most effective making your presence and involvement felt by being on your feet.

○ Adopt a composed stance. When addressing the class, stand up straight with shoulders relaxed and feet slightly apart. Avoid crossing your arms over your body, shifting weight from foot to foot or fiddling with jewellery, pens and so on.

○ Use the room. While whole-class exposition, recapping and so on is best done from the front of the class, try not to remain rooted to the spot for the duration of your lesson. Circulate – this works as a good class-management technique and also allows you to check understanding during a task.

BODY LANGUAGE – YOUR PRESENCE AND NON-VERBAL APPROACHES

Obvious as it may sound, remember to avoid turning your back to the class. This may be difficult if you are, for example, writing on the board, but it is important to keep a vigilant eye on your pupils if momentum is not to be lost. If possible, limit the use of huge chunks of board writing – not the best way to impart information anyway – by using prepared worksheets, for example. If it is unavoidable, either get into your class early to prepare your board writing, or write short sections at a time, returning your attention to the class at frequent intervals.

If a pupil is distracted/distracting, it is often more effective and less disruptive to mark their behaviour with a gesture or look than a verbal reprimand. The look with tilted head and slightly raised eyebrow is a classic of class management, and surprisingly effective. This can be extended to include auxiliary gestures which can further refine meaning. Other non-verbal signifiers can be used, such as the finger click, or simply moving closer to a pupil. It is quite possible to convey any number of points without words, from 'empty your mouth into the bin' to 'put down Julie's pen now' to 'what an astute observation, you clever little thing, you'. You will find what works best for you; the point is to let a pupil know that you are aware that they are off task, without disrupting the other pupils. The use of non-verbal expressions such as these suggest to the pupil a shared knowledge of what they *should* be doing, and that the strength of your vigilance and control is such that words are not needed.

While excessive and unfocused waving of arms can be distracting, gestures play an integral part in communication. Use your arms and hands to describe, emphasize and illustrate your points. For example, an open palm held up can indicate that you are presenting or sharing something. Counting gestures can be used to underscore key points. 'Pictures' of a description can be drawn with just a few well-placed motions of the hand.

Avoid threatening stances and gestures, even if you feel provoked. They can reveal that you have been affected on a personal level and can exacerbate rather than diffuse confrontation. Avoid actions such as pointing in a pupil's face; invading personal space; grabbing or poking, and so on. A simple raised hand with palm facing out towards the pupil and down can help diffuse a situation – more about this in Idea 50. You need to appear in control, even if you do not feel it.

Eye contact is a very important aspect of non-verbal communication. Be sure to maintain eye contact with your class in general and specific individuals in particular, as necessary. Scan the room when you are speaking, avoid looking at the same fixed point. Eye contact shows that you are engaging with, and aware of, your pupils and that you are confident in your role. Remember though, that you are not in a staring competition, and eye contact should be relaxed in the main, allowing you to use it to specific effect if needs be. Just the subtlest of changes in your glance can indicate a multitude of meanings.

BODY LANGUAGE – THE USE OF ARMS, HANDS AND EYE CONTACT

IDEA 41

VOICE

While body language is an undeniable element in effective communication, your voice remains perhaps your most valuable tool in the classroom. During a lesson, you may find yourself using your voice for a considerable amount of time and for a variety of purposes. As a key feature of your teaching, it is important therefore to focus on *how* you use your voice if it is to be used to its full potential.

○ As a general rule, your voice should be clear and loud enough to be heard by all, speech should be well paced, and you should use standard forms rather than colloquialisms. If your voice tends to be high pitched, practice lowering it – speaking more slowly can sometimes help with this.

○ Utilize a range of voices for different purposes. Your instructing voice should be different from your explaining voice, which should be different from your reprimanding voice, which should be different from your motivating voice, which should be different from your praising voice, which should be different from your questioning voice, and so on. This is not to suggest that you acquire a library of accents and impressions, but simply that you fit your voice to the particular purpose for which it is being used. This not only helps inject some variety into your teaching, but also provides verbal cues for your pupils, clarifying meaning, purpose and expected response.

○ Look after your voice. It is an invaluable tool. Avoid straining it and, obvious as it may sound, be sure to drink plenty of water during the day.

VOLUME CONTROL

A quiet voice can be used to great effect. Apart from maybe to gain attention – and this can be done by using a clap, for example – avoid raising your voice. Raising your voice frequently can diminish its status and, in turn, your status as speaker. Also, noise often breeds noise. Once you have the attention of the class, lower the volume a little. Encourage active listening in your pupils. IF SHOUTING IS YOUR DEFAULT RESPONSE IT WILL HAVE LITTLE EFFECT. JUST LIKE WRITING ONLY IN CAPITAL LETTERS, ANY IMPACT IT MAY HAVE IS LESSENED BY OVERUSE. Ahem.

It is quite common for trainees to feel that shouting is *the* response to inappropriate behaviour. This often results in a loss of voice and little actual difference in pupil behaviour. Once you have shouted, you leave yourself with little room to manoeuvre; you have played your trump card and have nowhere else to go.

Further, shouting, if it is your usual response, can become white noise and have little impact. Importantly, it also shows a pupil that they have provoked an emotional response from you and that you feel unable to control the situation by any other means. A shout can and does have a place in classroom management, but you owe it to your pupils, yourself, your larynx and your relationship with the class to use it sparingly and judiciously. On the whole, most low-level problems can be dealt with by calm repetition of instruction, for example, before they reach the stage where a vocal explosion is needed.

ESTABLISHING BOUNDARIES

In the initial phase in particular, it is important to be firm about your instructions. Avoid using the language or tone of *suggestion*; rather *tell* your class calmly what they are going to do. This can seem difficult for any number of reasons, but largely because of the potential clash between your silent desperation for the class to like you or at least do what you say and not make you feel like an idiot in front of other staff members, and their interest in seeing how malleable you are.

As mentioned previously, pupils actually like to know that there are firm boundaries governing what is and what is not acceptable in your lessons. They generally feel more secure when they know that you are in control of the lesson. Unfortunately, perhaps in order to establish this, some pupils will test out just where and how strong your boundaries are.

Acceptable and unacceptable behaviour in your lesson will, largely, be defined by school rules. Most schools will have a policy that deals with classroom behaviour and expectations – become familiar with it. If you have used your introductory lesson with a class to agree a set of rules, they will usually be a concise version of what is contained in the whole-school document. It is important that pupils understand what will not be tolerated in your classroom, and that they are also aware of any consequences for their behaviour. Again, sanctions should be in line with school policy.

It is almost inevitable that some pupils will push your boundaries to see if they collapse. These will usually be in the form of relatively minor misdemeanours, such as chewing gum or chatting. It is important that you act upon these quickly and calmly. By quickly enforcing a consistent chain of cause and effect, action and reaction, you will establish clear ground rules. It is a classroom truism that acting on minor transgressions will go some considerable way to lessening the likelihood of more persistent or significant misdemeanours occurring. By ensuring your pupils abide by your rules, you are asserting your authority in a simple and implicit way.

Your boundaries are not solely concerned with rules, but also with relationships. You should aim to have positive and productive relationships with your pupils, but remember that you are their teacher, not their peer. This can be a rather grey area for trainees, who may be keen to be liked and may also be relatively near the age of the pupils they teach. Also, the teacher–pupil relationship may be quite unlike any other you have experienced.

It can be very beneficial to share a joke with your class, and for you to share a warm, productive relationship. It remains important, however, for you and your pupils to remain aware of the nature of your relationship and its boundaries. You may observe teacher–pupil relationships that appear fairly relaxed, but try to remember that that member of staff has the luxury of familiarity and experience. This does not mean that you should squash your personality or individuality, but, certainly while you are establishing yourself, maintain a clear sense of your role and its parameters.

For example, while pupils will no doubt have a playground nickname for you, they should address you formally. Pupils should not feel free to have physical contact with you. The details of your private life should, in the main, remain just that and not be an available topic of discussion for your class. Your class, try as they might to find out, do not need your home address or telephone number. Pupils should not share their salacious or slanderous gossip about other members of staff with you. This is yet another balancing act for you to perform, but it is an important one. You must establish that, while you may be friendly, you are not their friend, but their teacher.

CONSISTENCY AND FAIRNESS

Closely tied in with establishing rules and boundaries are notions of consistency and fairness. Pupils often have an innate sense of justice (or injustice) when it comes to classroom behaviour and it is important that rules are applied consistently and fairly.

In most circumstances, each infringement of a classroom rule should be dealt with in the same way. If pupils see that Martin is allowed to keep his coat on, but Ishmael is not, then the rules themselves are undermined. There will, of course, be specific instances when rules and reactions need to be more fluid, but in the main you should aim to apply rules and sanctions consistently, even during last lesson on a Friday and when the rule breaker is twice your size. A minor infraction can become a significant problem as soon as the words 'Well, you didn't tell him' are uttered sullenly. Rules are there to provide a constant and solid foundation for learning and this is threatened if they are seen to be applied erratically.

Vigilance is important here. After all, you cannot act upon something of which you are unaware. Circulate during your lessons; this enables you to check understanding as well as behaviour. If you notice something, react to it in an appropriate manner. This leads neatly to fairness. Being consistent goes some way to ensuring that your class management is seen as fair. Your response also determines this further. Most minor transgressions are best dealt with by simply making the pupil aware that you have noticed, or issuing a warning look or word. Reprimands should focus on the behaviour rather than the pupil if they are to have maximum effect. If sanctions are to be used, they should be appropriate to the infringement.

A large part of good class management comes from a willingness to praise, encourage and reward. If there is no incentive to behave or work well, pupils can quickly become discouraged and disinclined to give of their best. Poor behaviour is often noted and disapproval voiced. This is quite right, but the converse should also occur. If a pupil offers an answer to a question, encourage them, even if the answer may not be the one you were looking for. If a class has worked hard and behaved well, praise them. Most pupils respond well to praise, and just as with the application of sanctions, praise should be used consistently and meaningfully. How this is offered will differ according to your own teaching style (although the coolness with which you correct behaviour should be replaced with more warmth and sincerity) and also the pupil or pupils involved. Some pupils might squirm with embarrassment at having their improved handwriting praised in front of the class, and might instead welcome a quiet acknowledgement of their achievement. Many schools have a merit or reward system in place – become familiar with it and use it effectively. This is not to suggest that pupils should in some way be bribed to behave well or work hard, but that, when they do, acknowledgement of this can act as a reinforcement of positive traits and attitudes. Praise, as with admonishment, should be specific to the action that has provoked it.

Sanctions, if they need to be used, should follow school policy. Get a copy of the policy and use it to inform your practice. Generally, pupils will be familiar with school sanctions and your actions will have more weight if they are consistent with those of the school. Again, you will need to ensure that you keep records and are organized in your awarding of sanctions. If you set a detention or give lines, you have to ensure that you remember or your system is undermined.

CONTENT, VARIETY AND PURPOSE – ENGAGING YOUR PUPILS

A vital aspect of classroom management is ensuring that your lesson is engaging, well pitched and has clear aims. Effective teaching can solve a great many class management problems. This is discussed in more detail in Idea 48 but engaging, varied and purposeful tasks can really help to ensure that much disruption is avoided. A significant amount of low-level classroom disruption can be brought about through boredom. Pupils who are not engaged with tasks will look for other things to do and ways in which to fill their time. When delivering a lesson aim for good pitch and task setting, appropriate pace, and a clear and sustained focus on learning.

It is good practice to ensure that your lessons have distinct phases and tasks that contribute to the whole. These may be, for example,

o settling–exposition–introductory
o task–elaboration–consolidation
o task–plenary–dismissal.

Lesson aims will influence the shape of your lesson, but variety should remain a feature. It is not uncommon to find trainees delivering lessons that have a 40-minute task in the middle. While this is sometimes unavoidable, it is not best practice in general. Many pupils, particularly younger ones, find it much easier to remain focused for shorter timed tasks or activities. Encourage active learning through your task setting. Pupils like to be engaged in purposeful activity – the unfocused and unoccupied pupil is far more likely to become distracted and distracting.

The following suggestions can be used or adapted as best fits your lesson.

o Clear objectives – pupils respond well to knowing *why* they are doing something. Make your aims and objectives clear and accessible, and reinforce them throughout your lesson.

o Try to include a variety of tasks and activities so as to engage different learning styles. A reading task could be followed by a group investigation and presentation; a writing task could be informed by Internet research and lead into a paired discussion – the permutations are endless. Try to think of inventive routes by which you can meet your objectives, while keeping a close watch on your aims.

o Pace – each section of your lesson should have a time limit. Remind pupils of timing as they work on task, while circulating to ensure that the time you have allowed is manageable.

o Recap and plenary – in most lessons it is advisable to check and reinforce understanding and achievement of aims at the end of the lesson. You can organize this as best fits your purpose, but it is good practice to afford pupils the chance to explain key features, skills or information by way of a plenary. You can guide this and also supplement it with a succinct recap that outlines what they have done during the lesson and where it has taken them.

o Resources – try to provide a variety of resources to aid the delivery of your lesson. These may be worksheets; IWB or PowerPoint presentations; pictures; audio, DVD or video recordings; modelling equipment, or any number of things. Well considered and presented resources can really help engage pupils' interest.

o Grouping – this is self-explanatory. Some tasks and objectives can benefit from well-managed pupil grouping. Just as some tasks will require individual, quiet application, others produce the best results when worked on by a group or a pair. Pupils often learn a great deal from explaining to, or exploring with, each other. Consider how best to utilize this in your lessons.

ON TASK AND OUT OF TROUBLE – TIPS FOR ENGAGING PUPILS IN LEARNING

59

DIFFUSING POTENTIAL CONFRONTATION

The majority of class management approaches and actions are relatively straightforward. Most disruption in class is low level and, if dealt with effectively, won't develop further. There may, however, come a time when more serious situations arise and it is imperative that you feel able to control them. Make sure that you are familiar with the school's systems and that you know the names of key members of staff. It helps to know who you should call on and how you should reach them, thereby providing yourself with a safety net.

The more challenging class management problems may involve a direct challenge to your authority, such as answering back, explicit refusal to follow a direct instruction, and so on. Alternatively, the confrontation may be between pupils. Each scenario requires a different response and will require you to react and subtly take control – common to all is the necessity to remain composed and professional throughout.

Sometimes, trainees are reluctant to call for help for fear of appearing incompetent. While the majority of class management issues will be within your control, some may require further assistance. Be sure to exercise judgement here – class management skills can only really develop through practising them, after all – but don't be afraid to get assistance if you feel a situation has become out of your control. Without wishing to be alarmist, it is a good idea to familiarize yourself with your legal position regarding matters such as separating pupils who are fighting and so on.

If a pupil is behaving in such a way as to clearly disrupt the learning of others it can be effective to point out, in a discreet manner, what is unacceptable and why. This minimizes the disruption and gives the pupil an opportunity to desist without the embarrassment that can lead to further escalation. If possible, intervention should not raise the ante.

Where possible, avoid the loud reprimand from the front of the class. This can serve to encourage resentment and retaliation. If possible, discuss the behaviour and disciplinary matters relatively privately. This prevents pupils from feeling that they are losing face.

Focus on the misdemeanour, not the pupil. Rather than 'You are a very rude child', try 'It is very difficult for anyone else to hear if you make noise'. Similarly, get the pupil to look at their behaviour rather than simply engage blindly in confrontation. Ask them what they were doing and, more importantly, why. Pupils often react without thinking their behaviour through. Encouraging them to do this can enable them to see the wider connotations or consequences of their actions.

It can sometimes be useful to phrase your wishes as choices. This can allow the pupils to feel that they are involved in decision making. Choices could be, for example, 'Put your headphones away or give them to me' or 'Work quietly where you are or move to sit by me'.

The choices will, of course, be between two courses of action that you have selected and are acceptable to you, but can nonetheless engender a feeling of participation and cooperation.

Don't be afraid to ask for assistance. Many teachers are reluctant to send for help for fear of appearing unable to control their class. While it is a good idea to deal with most situations yourself, sometimes you will need support. This is not a weakness. Send a responsible pupil to get assistance as per school procedure.

Confrontational situations between pupils will often be relatively easy to spot before they reach a physical stage. Act swiftly on any indications you pick up on. Separate pupils and quickly extinguish any provocative banter. Don't take sides or apportion blame at this point as it can often serve to further enflame the situation. It may be necessary to move a pupil out of the room. This should not be done as a matter of course, but can sometimes provide a cooling-off period. Again, follow school procedure for this. You do not want the problem to be simply displaced to the corridor.

It is often the case that in its grounds and corridors a school can seem a very different place. Here there is a multitude of pupils who are not under direct supervision. It can be a little intimidating to stroll through the school canteen or a main corridor at the start of break. The rules governing classroom behaviour don't seem to apply; you won't know most of the pupils around you, nor their relationships with one another, and you will feel somewhat uncertain of your role in this space, which is without the clear parameters of the classroom. But you remain a teacher even after you have left your lesson, and it is important that pupils see you as such.

Some schools have very structured and closely monitored systems governing movement through corridors, designated activity areas and canteen queues, and rules on where food and drink are to be eaten, and so on. If this is the case, ensure that you reinforce the system in place. If pupils are meant to be outside during lunch times, make sure that they are. If no food is to be brought into the school building or if pupils are expected to walk on the left, see that this is kept to. It is important that you follow and react to the same things as would any other teacher in the school. Between lessons, monitor the corridor as you wait for your class. During break and lunch times there are usually staff members on duty; nonetheless, should you encounter any misbehaviour, act upon it. This is not to suggest that you go looking for infringements and pounce eagerly upon the offending pupil, but rather that you show your awareness of school rules and your commitment to maintaining order.

The Pastoral Role

Schools organize their pastoral systems in a variety of ways, but most are based on a horizontal system. That is, forms are organized in year groups with a head of year overseeing each year. Some schools organize forms using a vertical system, whereby each form will be made up of a number of pupils from each year group. This is less commonplace however, because of the largely organizational complexities due to the sometimes incompatible needs of pupils of different ages. The degree of responsibility you have for your form as a trainee will differ from school to school. Generally, you will assist and support the existing form tutor. Nonetheless, the pastoral system can function as the heart of a school and it is important that you understand the structures and procedures by which it is run. These may include some of the following:

○ Find out when registration periods are and if there is a set routine.

○ Know who your head and deputy head of year are and where to find them.

○ During various points of the year, you may be expected to assist with matters such as collecting option choice forms or consent for inoculations. Be prepared.

○ Most schools use some form of pupil diary. Discover if and when you have to check them.

○ Sanctions, behaviour referrals and absence from lessons are sometimes passed through to the form tutor. Find out if they are for filing or action.

○ Familiarize yourself with any background information that may be available regarding your pupils.

○ Become acquainted with procedures and reasons for contacting a pupil's home.

○ Find out what systems are in place for sharing information about pupils. A form tutor can often be the member of staff with the most complete picture of a pupil as a whole. How is information gathered and used?

Being a form tutor can be something of a challenge. There are seemingly endless administrative tasks, a different relationship with pupils and distinctive responsibilities. Unlike the expertise in your subject that you will have developed through your education, very few of you will have had training or experience in the skills commensurate with this new role. Being a form tutor can, however, be a very rewarding and privileged position.

During the daily time spent with your form, you will really begin to understand what it means to multi-task. It is not uncommon to have to deal with issues as disparate as removing a pupil's jewellery, listening to a tearful tale of broken friendship and checking homework diaries. While doing all of this, you also have to take the register, collect absence notes and give out messages – all in a matter of minutes, too.

It is important therefore, to establish some kind of routine. Prioritize those things that *must* be done during the brief registration period. These will of course include taking the register and may also include any messages or notes that need to be passed on or given to you. Initiate uniform checks early on – you will generally find that once pupils understand that rogue items such as trainers and jewellery will not be tolerated then they quickly police themselves.

Many pupils feel most comfortable in their form room and you may well find yourself providing support and advice – more on this Idea 55. Much of this is not urgent and can be dealt with at a convenient time. However, if a pupil is distressed, make sure that you take a few minutes to speak with them. Arrange a time when you can speak at more length and in more depth if needs be.

You may also find yourself delivering some of the PSE programme. This is organized differently in every school. It can be a discrete series of lessons, complete with scheme of work and resources, or be more fluid. Whatever the arrangement, ensure that you are familiar with the topic(s) you may be delivering. Read any information given and, if possible, do a little homework too. Pupils may rely on you to provide them with up-to-date information. If you feel uncomfortable about delivering a given topic, such as sexual health, voice your concerns.

The varied work of a form tutor involves considerable administration functions, some of which may be subject to change due to recent workload developments. The most important of these is the daily register. A register is a legal document and it is important that it is completed accurately. As a general rule, do not mark a pupil as present unless you see them – even if you are assured by their friend that they are on an errand. Schools may use a paper or an electronic register but, whatever system is in place, make sure you become familiar with the codes used to denote various absences, such as a medical appointment or school trip.

An extension of register taking is taking in notes from pupils explaining absence. It can be useful to have a set routine for this – pupils may hand them to you when they arrive or you could collect them at the end of register taking, for example. In order to provide an accurate record, it is good practice to record the note in the register as soon as it is received. You should also file the notes away for possible future reference.

Other regular administrative tasks, such as checking homework diaries, can be organized efficiently using a set routine. Be sure to stick to it – checking only rarely can leave you with a daunting task and mean that important notes or comments may be missed. One-off tasks, such as collecting consent forms for vaccination or work experience, should be well ordered. Use a checklist to prevent the inevitable indignant cry of 'I gave it to you last week!'

ADMINISTRATIVE TASKS

One of the most rewarding (and exhausting, frustrating, infuriating, exasperating ...) aspects of teaching is the time spent with young people in a stimulating environment. The nature of teaching means that you are in close contact with young people day in and day out. It is important to remember that pupils don't come bubble-wrapped into school, but rather bring with them their own personalities, attitudes and experiences.

A form tutor will often be the person a pupil will turn to for help and support, and during your teacher training you may be faced with situations which require sensitive responses. These might come about through a direct approach from a pupil or through your own observations. In the main, pupils will simply need someone to talk to, or to ask for advice, but sometimes you may be privy to significant problems that will require you to call on assistance. If you have *any* concerns, inform the regular form tutor or head of year – they may have information of which you are unaware, or at least be able to provide the benefit of their experience. It is generally unwise to keep such matters to yourself. Each school should have a person who is designated with the responsibility for child protection issues. Find out who this is and report to them as soon as possible *any* suspicions or information you have that a child is suffering from, or at risk of, significant harm.

Be observant. As form tutor you will often be best placed to pick up any signs of difficulty. Look for any noticeable changes in the behaviour, appearance or attitude of your pupils, particularly if the shift is sudden, dramatic or prolonged. Ask a few casual questions and look for any developments.

Don't offer a pupil confidentiality. Pupils will often come to talk to you because they want a situation to change, but you need to be wary of assuring them that whatever they tell you will be in strict confidence. You have a duty to inform appropriate parties if a child is at risk.

Keeping a record. Make a dated record of your observations as soon after the event as possible. This can help you build up a more complete picture over time and enable you to identify any patterns. Be sure to keep any records secure, preferably not in your classroom, but if so locked away.

Bullying. Bullying is taken seriously by schools and your school should have a policy dealing with this issue. Offer the victim immediate practical support, but longer-term measures need to be put into place if the bullying is not to be repeated. Refer the matter to the head of year and follow the school's procedure.

Abuse. If a pupil approaches you with information regarding possible abuse, remember that yours is a listening role, not an investigatory one. You can offer discretion and support while the problem is investigated.

DEALING WITH SENSITIVE ISSUES

A form tutor is often a key link between home and school. You will be the one checking diaries for communications from parents and will often be the first point of contact should a parent feel concerned about their child. Pupils' home circumstances and arrangements will vary. Be sure that you are familiar with the home set-up. Parent–school relationships are a knotty and complex subject, much of which will not affect you directly during your training. As a trainee, you would be unwise to contact a pupil's guardians. Should an issue sufficiently merit concern, pass the matter on to your mentor, or the pupil's form tutor or head of year.

Much of the contact between school and home is of a fairly mundane nature – information regarding meetings or events, for example. There may, however, be instances when there is communication with home regarding a specific issue. Should you receive a letter from a parent, again, pass it on. While you *may* be asked to respond, you should not do so without the guidance and knowledge of the appropriate staff member. It is more usual for a more senior member of staff to respond on your behalf.

You are likely to be involved in a parents' evening during your training. As with all contact with parents, avoid personal comments about their child. Focus instead on tangible problems – for which you will have proof in the form of a mark book or behaviour referrals, for example – and look to forge solutions. Remember that if you offer to report back or investigate an issue, you *must* do so.

Also, remember that contact with home can be to point out achievement as well as to indicate concern. A letter or comment of praise can go a long way.

You will be involved in at least one parents' evening during your training. Your time with each parent will be brief, so it is important to create the right impression and to provide useful information in a succinct manner.

PARENTS' EVENINGS

○ Look the part! – You need to look professional. Be sure that you are smartly dressed. Carry yourself in a professional way. Sit up straight and look ready for business. Your desk should be clutter free and any documentation ready to hand. You are in a responsible position and parents will want you to look the part. They are entrusting their child's education to you after all.

○ Know the names of your pupils. This can be difficult if a parents' evening crops up in your first couple of weeks, but it is important. You need to be sure that you are talking about the right pupil. Take special notice in the lessons before a parents' evening – particularly if two pupils have a similar name.

○ Ensure that marking is up to date and that you have your mark book with you. Specific information is always better than vague generalizations, and can open discussion about targets. It may be useful to have examples of pupils' work with you, as it can clarify your comments.

○ Your comments should be constructive. Don't engage in a lengthy diatribe about a pupil. It doesn't go down well and this is not an opportunity for revenge, no matter how tempting it may seem.

○ Listen to parents. You may find out information which goes some way to explaining a pupil's attitude or attainment.

○ Stick to time limits. You will generally have around five minutes per parent and this needs to be kept to. If there is a genuinely pressing concern, offer to follow it up or arrange another meeting.

○ Both you and a pupil's parents share a common concern – the progress of their child. It is good practice to see the relationship as a partnership, rather than adversarial. Similarly, some parents find school environments intimidating. Don't flummox them with a private language of education-speak. They want to understand how their child is doing and how progress can be made.

As already stated, much of your contact with parents will be fairly routine. There may, however, be instances where a meeting is called to discuss a pupil's unsatisfactory progress, behaviour or attitude. While you will not be expected to face these sorts of meeting alone – and indeed you should always seek advice when approached by parents – they can nonetheless feel very intimidating. Again, in most cases, parents will be concerned about their child's progress, too, and the meeting will pass productively.

It is important to approach meetings of this nature with an emphasis on partnership. That is, rather than the parent feeling that they have been dragged into school to hear how dreadful their child is, there should be a clear sense of both parties getting together to work out strategy rather than apportion blame. Be welcoming and non-threatening in your manner. Try to open conversation with a neutral or positive discussion that helps to establish a relationship. Don't immediately wade in with a list of complaints about their child. Be sure to have evidence to hand regarding the particular problem, along with any documentation relating to sanctions and strategies that have been tried. Work out solutions that involve school and home. Agree on a course of action, and send a copy to parents following the meeting. Be sure that you are never left to hold a meeting of this nature alone, and also that you are informed about any mitigating factors prior to the meeting.

Assessment and Marking

ASSESSMENT – WHAT IS IT FOR?

Assessment of pupils' work can often feel as daunting for the trainee teacher as for the pupil. There is the need to be sure about what you are assessing and why; whether you have chosen the most effective assessment method; what feedback you are going to provide; your familiarity with level or grade criteria; and your consistency and accuracy in applying criteria to pupils' work.

It is not unusual for trainee teachers to understand assessment as being end-of-unit summative examinations or extended pieces of writing that are levelled or graded. While this kind of assessment plays a significant part in judging pupil progress and understanding, it is only one of a number of different kinds of assessment that take place. Indeed, much of what goes on in the average lesson assesses learning in one way or another. Question and answer sessions, plenaries, successful task completion, self-assessment activities and so on all encourage pupils to reveal their understanding, which is then acted upon in one way or another.

Assessment allows you to gauge understanding and progress, set targets for further progress and plan your lessons so as to best facilitate this. The different types of assessment will generally be *of* measuring understanding; or *for* focusing on improvement and learning, although, of course, they are rarely wholly exclusive. Assessment can be short, medium or long term and will become an integral part of your teaching and your pupils' learning, while also enabling you to provide information regarding a pupil's progress to a number of interested parties such as parents, heads of department, other teachers, support assistants and of course the pupils themselves.

It is important to realize that not all assessment is effective. There is the risk of demotivating pupils who routinely receive low grades or negative comments. So before undertaking assessment think about the following:

O What are you hoping to achieve?
O What type of assessment is appropriate for the task (see Idea 62 for types of assessment)?
O How will you link the assessment to targets and achievements?
O How will the assessment help the pupil to improve their skills?
O Will your assessment take the form of grades or comments?
O How will you ensure that your comments or grades are positive rather than dismissive?
O How will you evaluate the extent of the learning which has taken place?

DEVELOPING EFFECTIVE ASSESSMENT

Assessment is an essential part of teaching and learning. It can be for a variety of purposes, provide a range of information for a number of parties and, as such, can take many forms. Before assessing your pupils, it is important for you to consider what it is you are testing, and what will be rewarded before deciding what kind of assessment to set your pupils. The following is a glossary to help you understand a few of the types of assessment and the terms used to describe them. Clearly, some of the assessment types outlined below will be used daily, while others may be used far less frequently. Some may be administered by you, others by the school and others by outside agencies. Also, most forms of assessment will fit more than one category.

- ○ **Informal, short-term assessment.** During your lessons, you will be assessing pupils' learning in a variety of ways. For example, you will ask questions that may test knowledge, understanding, analysis and evaluation. You may use short tests – oral or written – in class. Pupils may provide feedback or take part in a plenary. Also, your written or verbal feedback provides pupils with targets and some sense of their progress.

- ○ **Summative assessments.** These test learning, usually at the end of a topic or unit, and of course at end-of-year school or national examinations. These types of assessments are assessments of learning, though the information they provide is often used to inform future teaching and learning.

- ○ **Formative assessments.** These types of assessment are used to set targets for learning and identify needs.

- ○ **Teacher assessments.** These are assessments made using the National Curriculum level descriptions. They are made supplementary to the national tests at KS1 and 2.

- ○ **National Curriculum tests.** Pupils in England take these national tests in the core subjects (mathematics and English only at KS1) at the end of each Key Stage. They are then awarded a level on the basis of their performance.

o **Norm referenced.** This means that a pupil's attainment is judged in comparison to others on a sliding scale; for example, the top 10 per cent being awarded a particular grade, the next 10 per cent the grade below and so on.

o **Criterion referenced.** This means that attainment is judged on a pupil by pupil basis and is assessed by reference to set criteria.

o **CAT tests and reading tests.** These types of tests assess pupils' abilities and skills in key areas. Pupils in many schools sit these tests in Year 7. Cognitive Ability tests measure reasoning skills in the areas of verbal reasoning, quantitative reasoning and non-verbal reasoning. Reading tests offer a reading score or age for a pupil based on their ability to read words and sentences of increasing complexity. Pupils' scores in these tests are often used to predict potential grades at KS3 and KS4.

ASSESSMENT FOR LEARNING

As already outlined, assessment is not just *of* learning – an endpoint where achievement is simply measured or judged against set standards. Rather, it is part an ongoing process and informs future teaching and learning.

Assessment *of* learning is summative, that is it tests the skills or knowledge a pupil has amassed, often at the end of a unit, year or Key Stage, and judges attainment. Assessment *for* learning is formative, that is it focuses on using assessment to inform progress. This will, of course, often entail using information gathered from summative assessment in a formative way.

Using assessment to inform future progress can be undertaken in myriad ways, some of which will be subject-specific. The following points or tips can be used or applied as and when appropriate, but they should help provide a basis for effective use of assessment for learning. It is important to remember that these ideas must be used specifically and purposefully. For example, don't just ask pupils to swap books and say what they think about a classmate's work; apart from the social problems this may cause, it is rather a vague instruction. Give pupils something specific to look for, a simplified mark scheme perhaps, and encourage them to suggest tips for improvement, rather than to judge or rank. Similarly, self assessment can be a very effective learning tool, but is quite pointless if it is an unfocused, tagged-on exercise. Pupils will need to have guidelines and goals, which are reviewed and developed, if self assessment is to be truly productive.

Give your pupils clear, specific and meaningful targets that are reviewed and amended. Explain not only what they have to do, but also what they will learn by doing it. Share pupil-friendly learning objectives and assessment criteria, and use exemplar material to illustrate how grade/level criteria are used to mark a piece of work. Show them example responses and model answers. Let them know *explicitly* what they need to do to reach the next level. Give pupils frequent opportunities to self assess, identify strengths and set goals. Encourage pupils to read and act upon comments made on their marked work, and promote well-managed peer assessment.

Well-judged questions can be effective short-term assessment tools. Pupil responses can tell you a lot about what they have understood, the depth of understanding, and how they can use that understanding. Low-level, information-based questions can help you assess retention of facts, but higher-level questions can assess and help to develop more complex skills. Try to include questions that encourage pupils to make links or comparisons between concepts or ideas; to infer and to surmise; or to transfer new skills or knowledge to different arenas.

Use the findings of any assessment (formal or informal) to inform your planning. Identify strengths that can be developed further and devise tasks and strategies to address needs. Differentiate in approach, task and resource to meet the learning needs of different pupils.

Regarding the learning environment, promote a productive and positive atmosphere where pupils feel part of the learning process. Focus on improvement rather than judgement alone, and encourage pupils to become increasingly involved in and responsible for their own learning.

Marking can be a heavy burden on an already unwieldy workload. It is important for you and for your pupils that your marking is purposeful and well managed. Your pupils will need to know how they are doing and what they can do to improve, and you will need to feel confident that you are facilitating this. The following may be more applicable for some subjects or tasks than others, but most can be adapted.

○ Familiarize yourself with school and departmental policy for marking. You may find that books have to be taken in at given intervals; that a certain colour of pen is specified; that school- or department-wide margin symbols are used to denote errors; that grades, marks or levels are used in particular places and ways, or that there are guidelines for writing comments.

○ Be aware of the purpose of the task and of your assessment of it. Some pieces of work will require detailed feedback and target setting, or may focus on a specific skill or area. Have a specific and explicit assessment focus and mark accordingly – for your sanity and that of your pupils. Marking every piece of work for every possible mistake or outcome is hugely time consuming, just as a mess of red pen can be very discouraging for pupils.

○ In the main, try to avoid simply ticking the bottom of each page. Make notes or comments in the body of the text. This can be useful as a means of giving pupils a more complete and specific picture of what they need to focus on, and what they have done well, as well as showing that you have engaged with their work.

As already stated, a heavy marking load can be difficult to manage and can tip you into a cycle of unmarked work, difficulties with your lessons as a result, and then more unmarked work. While marking is an unavoidable part of teaching and you will have to spend countless evenings in marking work when you would rather be anywhere else, you can lessen the load a little:

○ Mark pupils' work regularly. Get into the habit early on of marking work frequently. Marking a week's work is more manageable and productive than being faced with a mountain of unmarked books.

○ While all work should have some feedback, it doesn't always have to be written, nor does it always have to be from you. Oral responses are suitable for some tasks and pupils should be given opportunities to respond to their own work and the work of their peers.

○ Organize your marking timetable and think ahead. If you know you are about to have a set of GCSE coursework essays to mark, it may not be the best time to set your deadline for your Year 8 class to give in their projects.

○ If a piece of work has a narrow or specific focus, and is, in the main, a summative assessment, grids or other highlighting devices can be used to show where the objective has been met. You may even assess only a particular aspect of a piece of work. It is not always practical or productive to mark every piece of work for everything.

○ The purpose of the work set will guide the response given. If the work is a short class exercise it will require a different response to a more involved end-of-unit assessment piece. Mark accordingly.

MANAGING YOUR MARKING LOAD

MARKING FOR PUPILS

Pupils generally look for a grade or mark first before reading comments – if they read them at all. Try to encourage them to focus on what you have written. You might put grades or marks on a separate page, grade only certain pieces of work or set up a system where pupils have to show in the next piece that they have taken on board your advice. Your comments should be part of a dialogue between you and the pupils, and as such need to be responded to in order to be effective.

When setting work, be absolutely certain that pupils understand what is required of them and what will be looked for when you mark their work.

Your feedback should, in general, provide a summative comment along with specific targets for improvement. Comments such as 'Well done' or 'Good' are not very useful by themselves. These will vary in detail and length according to the nature and purpose of the task. Be professional, positive and clear in your language and tone.

Mark work regularly and to return it to pupils swiftly. This is important for a number of reasons. Pupils want to see how they have done; they want to feel that you are interested in their work; it allows them to act upon targets while the task is still relatively fresh in their minds; it allows you to have a more complete picture of pupils' progress; and can act as a class management device too.

Mark schemes are used to evaluate pupil achievement according to standardized criteria. For the bulk of your marking, you may find that you do not use a mark scheme as such, but rather focus on individual targets. Many trainees find mark schemes provide a kind of raft upon which they can place their judgements, others find that interpreting and applying the mark scheme confidently can be daunting.

Mark schemes may be used for a variety of purposes and come from a range of sources. You may use a departmental scheme to assess an end of unit test or task, or use an examination board mark scheme to mark mock GCSE papers, for example. The subject and task being assessed will, of course, determine the nature of the mark scheme. Some may indicate tightly defined right or wrong answers, while others may provide quite complex guidance regarding how to interpret any possible responses.

When using a mark scheme for those responses that are not short and factual, be sure to highlight the key features that you need to look out for. Many words or phrases are repeated, so highlight those that *specifically* identify or mark out one grade or mark from another. It may be the difference between 'recognizing' and 'interpreting' a given feature. Remember that you are not looking for a 'perfect' response, but one which fits the given criteria. It is quite possible for a pupil to receive full marks for an answer. If a response has fulfilled all of the criteria for a mark or grade, look to see if any of the features of the next grade or mark up are present. A pupil doesn't have to do *everything* in a given grade boundary to be awarded it. Reward what is there, rather than penalize what isn't.

Be consistent within your own interpretation and application of a mark scheme. If you are consistently three marks too harsh, it isn't really a problem; your marks can be adjusted accordingly and it shows some clear awareness in application. If you are sometimes ten marks too severe, sometimes two and sometimes six marks too lenient, then there is a problem that is more difficult to disentangle. Agonizing over marks is common to all teachers, particularly when you are starting out. Ask for advice, and see if you could sit in on moderation or be given exemplars of marked work.

SECTION 7

Differentiation

UNDERSTANDING DIFFERENTIATION

Differentiation means the modifying of your teaching so as to meet the various learning needs of your pupils. Differentiation is a vital element of your teaching if all pupils are to meet their various potentials. It is also very time consuming and complicated and sometimes takes a back seat to the many other pressing demands.

Even if pupils are in sets, there may still be a surprisingly wide range of abilities within the group, of a general or more specific nature. The three most commonly identified ways in which you can differentiate are: by task – setting pupils different tasks according to ability; by support – providing support by way of LSAs or material; and by outcome – providing tasks that are accessible to all pupils, but which will be differentiated by level of response. There is, however, some debate as to the efficacy of differentiation by outcome alone. Broadly, effective differentiation tends to take place through content or task; that is, *what* we expect our pupils to learn and *how* we expect them to learn, rather than how well they manage a task.

While differentiation is too large, and perhaps contentious, a topic with too many variables to be discussed in full here, the following pointers can provide a practical basis for your consideration of how best to facilitate the learning of all of your pupils.

In order to plan for differentiation effectively, the starting point should be a survey of available data on pupils. This can include SAT results; IEPs or ILPs; CAT scores; reading test results; information from primary schools, LSAs and other teachers, and so on. While it is unrealistic to expect each teacher to undertake an exhaustive research project on each pupil, this being more of a whole-school issue, do try to use whatever information is made available to you as it saves time and increases the effectiveness of your lessons.

When preparing worksheets and resources, try to make sure that your font is large and clear. Also, avoid overcrowding as this can obscure focus and lead to confusion.

Use writing frames, models and clearly structured worksheets to help support and structure writing and investigatory tasks. Provide models or sentence starters and break down longer tasks into shorter, more manageable stages. Rather than simply ask more able pupils to do 'more of the same', give them extension tasks that build on what they have done, and that develop knowledge or skills.

Set regular, achievable, specific, short-term targets which can be monitored easily. Praise achievement when a target is met. Have high expectations. Similarly, set tasks which pupils can complete in the time given.

PLANNING FOR DIFFERENTIATION

DIFFERENTIATION IN THE CLASSROOM

The following are suggested strategies that you can try in the classroom depending on the needs of the pupils. They are rather broad but should at least provide a springboard for more individual support.

○ Establish a regular organizational pattern covering aspects such as entrances and exits; seating arrangements; where work is kept; question protocol, and so on. Within this basic framework, lessons can, and should, be varied, but a basic established pattern helps pupils concentrate.

○ Use your voice. Adopt different specific tones of voice for various aspects of your lesson such as instructing, explaining, getting attention, and so on. It helps act as a verbal signpost.

○ Avoid long-winded instructions. Try to make instructions clear, short and to the point, asking pupils to rephrase to check understanding. As a general rule, do not give more than two or three instructions at a time.

○ Set questions which allow pupils to achieve something. For example, have some 'spotting' questions as part of comprehension exercises or allow those pupils who are least confident to give their answers first in group activities. Frame questions so that they get progressively more difficult or involve more sophisticated answers, and provide guidance/support or allow pupils to answer in pairs.

○ Avoid over-reliance on writing. Visual learners respond well to illustrations, graphs, colour coding and so on to record or remember ideas. Similarly, some pupils respond well to practical, 'doing' tasks, and others still prefer tasks that are based on speaking and listening. Try to include a variety of teaching and learning styles in your lessons.

During your training, and throughout your career, you will teach pupils for whom English is an additional language. Each pupil's degree of familiarity with English will vary, as will the literacy level in his or her first or other language. Each child in your class should have access to the curriculum and be afforded opportunities for learning. This can appear quite daunting if you and your pupil share few common words, but a little effort and preparation can produce rewarding results for both you and your pupils.

o Planning and preparation – Find out what support systems are in place in your school and make use of them. Many schools have designated EAL support staff – avail yourself of their experience and knowledge. Be sure not to confuse a pupil's language needs with a lack of ability. Find out as much as is available regarding education history, aptitudes and so on. If practicable, produce differentiated worksheets that allow the pupils to participate in the lesson. Use group and pair work in your lessons. Plan tasks that are supported throughout. Use visual aids, sound, demonstration and so on in your lessons.

o During the lesson – Be sure to address your pupil by name (correctly pronounced) and to give yours clearly; write it down if needs be. Be sure that your pupils can see you clearly and that they are not seated alone. Much understanding during the early stages of language acquisition may come from body language, facial expression and demonstration. Give pupils the opportunity to participate in everyday classroom activities, such as handing back books. Provide scaffolding and support for tasks – oral as well as written. Be sure that you speak clearly and don't rush explanations. Check understanding frequently and give each pupil the chance to accomplish something. In some instances, it may be most efficacious for some pupils to use their first language – when they are discussing difficult concepts, for example. Learning doesn't *have* to be done in English. Unless you share a language with the pupil, be sure that they are supported by EAL staff or by a peer. Make your classroom a positive environment where difference is valued. Use multicultural display materials and references. While many pupils who are not first language speakers of English may initially be withdrawn, be sure that you address them and include them while they go through what is, after all, a significant adjustment.

Schools may organize pupils for learning in a number of ways. Classes may be set for each subject; set only for certain subjects or in KS4 only; pupils may be banded or streamed, or pupils may be taught in mixed-ability classes throughout the curriculum and age range.

For many trainees, the mixed-ability lesson seems to be the most difficult to prepare and deliver. While it is worth remembering that all classes are mixed ability to some degree, the range of abilities in some classes can be intimidating. The clear focus on teaching and learning that you employ in your lessons as a matter of course – including factors such as variety of task types, clear objectives and instructions and so on – will go some considerable way to ensuring that your teaching of mixed-ability classes is effective. Combined with this, the following tips may help you to feel a little more confident:

o Prepare yourself. Be aware of the range and types of ability you can expect to find in your class.
o Have staggered desired learning outcomes: that is, what *all* pupils should be expected to have learned, what *most* should have learned and what *some* should have learned.
o Use a variety of types of pupil grouping, dependent on task. Sitting pupils of a given ability level together may be suitable for some tasks, but not for others. You don't want to create a ghetto or sets within the class, and peer learning can be very effective for all concerned.
o Make sure that learning objectives are achievable and differentiated.
o Set explicit learning targets that assess a pupil's individual progress against their own prior attainment – ipsative assessment.

THE MIXED-ABILITY CLASSROOM

○ Make sure that all pupils have the opportunity to participate in question and answer sessions. Insist on hands up and select the pupil who will give the answer.

○ Homework can be differentiated according to need. For example, some pupils may perform tasks that consolidate and reinforce the knowledge and skills they have learned in class, while others may apply that knowledge in a different context.

○ Remember that whole-class teaching is not the whole story of a lesson. You will spend time teaching pupils in groups or individually. These times can be useful for providing extra support or extension.

○ Avoid simply giving more able pupils more work to do. This doesn't really help them to develop. Instead, try to give them tasks that test or develop higher-level skills.

○ Tasks and skills can be developed along a continuum moving from simple to abstract, and supported to independent.

○ Remember that you are teaching the whole class, not a selected group. There can be an understandable tendency to address the highest achieving pupils and those that struggle the most. Another tendency is to 'teach to the middle'. All of your pupils need to play an equal part in your lessons.

ICT as a Tool for Teaching and Learning

As part of your teaching practice you will be expected to show that you can use ICT to enhance learning. This includes the use of ICT outside the classroom in, for example, your record keeping and resource creation. Opportunities should be given for pupils to use ICT to support their learning in all subjects. As a general rule, you should be able to demonstrate the effective use of ICT in both your teaching *and* your pupils' learning; that is, for example, in your presentation and preparation and their active engagement with ICT so as to meet learning aims and objectives. Make sure that you check subject-specific suggestions and guidelines. Statutory requirements aside, ICT can be a massively successful and, yes, exciting aid in the classroom, both as a presentational tool and as an interactive learning aid.

It is important to remember that not all lessons will be better delivered using PowerPoint or the IWB, and that ICT is used most effectively when it is used as a resource, not as the lesson itself. It is also worth noting that ICT isn't just about computers and software packages, but includes, for example, the use of film, digital cameras, sound and so on. The following Ideas 76 to 79 are by no means a comprehensive list of suggestions, but may provide some pointers for those who have yet to explore the possibilities afforded by ICT in the classroom.

That the Internet is an invaluable research tool for pupils and teachers alike goes without saying. What needs to be remembered is that the Internet alone is simply a tool and its effective use in the classroom requires specific guidance and aims. The too easily available plethora of coursework essays and unsavoury sites aside, Internet research can end up as an inefficient trawl through endless pages with little actual focus.

When using the Internet with a class, the same rules should apply as they would to any lesson – clear and specific aims and objectives should be the sustained focus. For example, to maintain the focus of the class and help keep their twitchy fingers away from games and ring tones, give pupils *specific* sites to search for *particular* information. If you are researching a broad topic, arm your pupils with the addresses of sites you have already checked for suitability, and task sheets that can only be completed using information found on directed websites. This also allows for differentiation as pupils can be directed to different sites and search for information of varying degrees of complexity. Make sure, too, that the information is then *used* for a purpose – group presentations or comprehension, for example – rather than being an end in itself. There is sometimes a tendency for lessons such as these to be a little lacking in direction and, therefore, real purpose.

The Internet cannot take the place of a well-planned lesson. What it can do is provide an effective resource for that well-planned lesson to succeed. Research and selection of information can also be used to refine strategies for the seeking of information. Pupils can edit and refine searches to ensure they arrive quickly at the information they need or websites can be grouped together thematically.

DRAFTING AND EDITING

Word processing packages can enable pupils to edit and resequence text efficiently. This in turn can enable pupils to make editing decisions which explore style, meaning and structure. Texts can be transformed to meet the needs of different audiences and purposes, and spelling and grammar checks can help improve accuracy.

This is not to suggest that word processing is not without its problems. Pupils often use word processing simply to produce a 'best' copy of an essay or piece of work. While this is an advantage, it is not the most efficient use of ICT. The real worth of word processing lies in its flexibility. Pupils should use ICT to enable them to redraft and edit meaningfully, rather than simply as a typewriter. This can be practised by, for example, giving pupils sequencing or editing tasks as part of their study of a text.

Pupils need to be made aware of the limitations of spelling and grammar checkers. While these features are valuable tools, they do not do away with the need for accurate spelling. Many spelling mistakes, especially of words that sound alike, may not be picked up.

Word processing can also be used effectively in the creation of collaborative texts, where groups of pupils construct a text as a combined effort. This will mean saving and retrieving work from common folders, but it can be very effective.

Packages such as Publisher can provide pupils with the means to transform texts and produce work that is well presented and in keeping with text type. Pupils can produce newspaper front pages, create leaflets for a local attraction or an advert, using images and text. As with any tasks of this nature, the focus must remain on the learning objective for your lesson. Ensure that pupils are furnished with sufficient knowledge about the texts they will transform and create before they begin.

DESKTOP PUBLISHING

PRESENTATION AND INTERACTION

Presentational tools such as PowerPoint can be very effective in the classroom. As a teacher, you can present ideas and key points clearly and without turning your back to the class.

Many pupils respond well to the use of image, colour and sound that is available in presentations of this kind. Avoid using too much writing in your presentation – key points should be flagged up with further information provided through talk.

PowerPoint can be used interactively, too. Clicking on the barely visible triangle that presents itself on the bottom left-hand corner of each slide enables you to change the pointer to a pen. This can be used by you or by pupils to annotate text, for example. The interactive whiteboard (IWB) can allow pupils to interact with text in an immediate and creative way. It allows pupils to transform, create, explore, organise, analyse, modify, model and engage with concepts and tasks directly.

The Wider Picture

There is a huge body of legislation relating to teaching. Much of it changes completely or is amended with some frequency. Fortunately, a relatively small fraction of this has any significant impact on the day-to-day duties and responsibilities of the classroom teacher. The following is by no means a comprehensive account of the law as it pertains to teaching and teachers, but is a distillation of some key features:

○ 'Duty of Care'. Teachers have a duty to care for the well-being of pupils in their charge as would a responsible parent. This means taking reasonable steps and precautions to prevent injury or harm from objects or persons. This includes any defective fixtures and fittings in the school premises. Breaching this duty can result in charges of negligence should a child come to harm.

○ Schools can keep pupils in detention once parents have been given 24 hours' notice. Permission does not have to be given but notice does. However, be sure to stick closely to school policy on such matters.

○ While it should really be a very last resort, *reasonable* physical force *can* be used by a teacher to restrain a pupil so as to prevent that pupil causing harm to themselves or others. Pupils may also be restrained physically if they are damaging property or behaving in such a way as to jeopardize discipline. It is important to remember, however, that as a general rule, physical contact with pupils is to be avoided.

○ Teachers can confiscate inappropriate items, such as cigarette lighters or mobile phones from pupils but cannot keep them indefinitely. Most schools will have a policy relating to the return of various confiscated items.

There is, of course, much more that could be said regarding your position as a teacher vis-à-vis the law. Most school policies regarding issues such as health and safety, sanctions and so on have been written with legal responsibilities very much in mind, and so abiding by these will often help ensure that you abide by your legal responsibilities.

Your teaching practice really is a time of opportunity – even if it may not always seem that way. You have the chance to learn about and involve yourself in all aspects of school life. Rather than being a ghostly figure that appears during lesson times and then shuffles off, try immersing yourself in school life beyond the walls of your teaching room.

Involvement in extra-curricular activities can mean a whole host of things from playing tuba in the school orchestra to going on a residential field trip to helping with the rugby team. Whatever your interests or proclivities, this kind of involvement really can enhance your school experience in a number of ways. You spend time with pupils away from the classroom and can learn new things about them and develop different kinds of relationships; you meet pupils who you may otherwise never have spent time with, facilitating an activity they have *chosen* to spend their time doing – this can give you many kudos points; you work with a wider variety of staff members, often outside your own subject area; you can gain a more complete picture of your school, its ethos and what it provides alongside the National Curriculum.

There are practical, perhaps cynical, reasons for this, too. As outlined in Section 1, one of the Standards for QTS is Professional Values and Practice. Your involvement in the school production, your coaching of the Year 7 football team or your assisting with a lunch time club can act as evidence of your contribution to the whole school community. Also, your school will, after all, provide a reference for you and the time you selflessly gave up can really help your profile.

GETTING INVOLVED

TRIPS AND CLUBS

As already discussed, getting involved in extra-curricular activities can be an important and enjoyable part of your teaching practice. Generally, you will find yourself assisting with clubs, trips and projects that are overseen and organized by other staff members. Nonetheless, you will need to be sure that any activity you supervise is well-managed and safe. Without wishing to strip away your enthusiasm, it is worth bearing the following points in mind.

A safe and well-organized trip or club is one that can then be enjoyed to the full. As a trainee, you will not have responsibility for organizing a school trip, though you may well find yourself assisting. Every school trip has to be risk assessed. Trip leaders need to be aware of any potential safety issues and the first aid competencies of assisting staff. Adventure activities should not be undertaken unless they can be staffed by those assessed as competent in the activity and in any emergency procedures that may need to be implemented.

Trips should have an educational objective and should be well-organized and researched. Parents should be given full information on the trip and what it will entail before they give consent, including any medical information and consent to treatment.

If you are to be put in charge of a small group, be sure to have a list of names and, if possible, contact numbers. Set up a fixed meeting point where you can be reached if appropriate. Be sure that you are familiar with any needs – medical or other – of any of the pupils in your charge. Remember that you are there as a member of staff.

If assisting or running a club, be sure that you keep a record of its members. Be aware of any health and safety issues, as well as any statutory requirements, such as first aid proficiency or coaching awards. Be sure that your club is well-organized and focused, rather than just a place for pupils to hang out if it's raining. If any equipment is needed, be sure that you have a safe place in which to store it.

Following from recommendations made in, among others, the 2001 White Paper 'Schools – Achieving Success' and the subsequent 2002 Green Paper '14–19: Extending Opportunities, Raising Standards', the policy document '14–19: Opportunity and Excellence' and the Tomlinson report developments regarding a 'coherent 14–19 phase' have been very much in the news. All of these documents can be accessed via the Internet. There has been considerable heated debate regarding the proposals and the government's rejection of Tomlinson's proposals, and you should make it your business to explore the debates. The following digest provides a useful overview as to how the developments outlined in the White Paper may affect practice in schools and colleges.

While opting to maintain distinct academic and vocational options and pathways, the Paper proposes more variety of opportunity and an increased focus on vocational qualifications. More young apprenticeships will be available to pupils. In 14 key subjects, specialist diplomas – linked to key sectors – will be available to pupils. This will start in 2008, with four subject areas – ICT, creative and media, health and social care, and engineering – until 2015, when all 14 will be in place. Pupils will need to obtain a C grade in mathematics and English in order to pass their diploma. As a further part of the increased focus on vocational qualifications, there are plans for 200 vocationally orientated schools to be established by 2008. While these new programmes will not be available in every school or college, provision should be available in each region. A new science GCSE has been timetabled for introduction in 2006, and there is to be increased focus on improving standards in mathematics and English. The most able A-level students will be tested by more demanding supplementary questions as well as a 4,000-word extended essay. They may also be able to follow some university modules. Universities will also have access to the students' marks for individual A-level modules, as opposed to a single grade.

IDEA
84

STRESS

While teaching is an undoubtedly rewarding occupation, it also features regularly at the top of stressful occupations list. Stress affects not only your professional performance, but also your personal life and well being too. Symptoms are often very individual, but may include disturbed sleep patterns; fatigue; forgetfulness and poor time keeping; over reaction to everyday incidents or pressures; a feeling of not being in control; increased susceptibility to illness; and the deterioration of personal relationships

There is a responsibility for stress to be dealt with at an institutional level, rather than it simply being up to individual teachers to deal with it themselves. Stress is caused by different things, presents itself in different ways, and can be dealt with in various ways. What is important, if you recognize that you are suffering from stress, is that you act upon it. Stress is not a failing, and needs to be acted upon early. Don't just hope that your feelings will go away. Take a deep breath and take action. Try to identify what may be causing or exacerbating your stress. Often, there may not be a specific cause, but a general sense of being unable to cope. Nonetheless, by recognizing that you are stressed and acting upon it, you are regaining some control. Talk to someone who can offer practical assistance or be a sympathetic sounding board. If the root cause is school related, your mentor, tutor or a colleague may be able to help ease the specific problem, if one exists, or at least relieve some of the pressure you feel under.

The following suggestions are not a prescription for your well being, but may provide ideas that may go some way to helping you feel more in control.

o Keep some time for you. Teaching is very time consuming, and can eat up all of your waking hours if you let it. Remember to spend some time doing whatever it is that you find relaxes you. While it is good to get things off your chest, avoid spending your social time talking about school.

o Exercise. As clichéd as it sounds, physical exercise really can help reduce stress levels. It can take whatever form best suits you – walking your dog, playing football or taking dance classes – but try to take some time out to keep fitness levels up.

o Some people find it useful to write down what is bothering them. Writing can often help you get a clearer perspective on things, as the process and organization help distance you from your concerns. Make a *short* list of actions you may take to deal with various problems.

o Be realistic. Unrealistically high demands and standards benefit no one. Look at what you can expect to achieve in a given time period and stick to it. Similarly, try to keep your breaks for yourself as far as possible and avoid saying 'yes' to everything.

o Don't ignore symptoms. If you feel fatigued or ill, look after yourself. Dragging yourself in to school is not always for the best in the long run.

The Hunt Begins –
Looking For
Employment

IDEA

86

INDUCTION

You have successfully completed your training, are a member of the GTC and have a special teacher number, just for you. Now comes the next stage – your induction year. The induction period is compulsory for those who wish to teach in maintained schools. During your induction period, you have to demonstrate, in your day-to-day teaching, that you are continuing to meet the Standards for QTS and the National Induction Standards. You will need to show that you are progressing and developing from the base of your teacher training. Schools organize induction in different ways, but the following are general guidelines as to what to expect.

Each school will have a member of staff with designated responsibility for NQTs. You will have an induction programme – based in large part on your CEDP – which may include observing experienced teachers, INSET and so on. Each programme will be specific to that particular NQT. You will have a reduced timetable (no more than 90 per cent of a full timetable) so as to facilitate your induction. Your progress should be reviewed half-termly, and will usually focus on your progress as indicated by your everyday work rather than the more formal checklist assessments you encountered during your teacher training. The headteacher of your school, acting upon evidence and advice regarding your progress, will then make a recommendation as to whether you will pass your induction.

The induction period for NQTs is no fewer than three full terms. If you are on a part-time contract, your induction period must still cover the same number of sessions. You can complete your induction in more than one school, as long as you work in each school for at least one term. There is no time limit as to when induction starts, although it is expected that it will be completed within five years of its initiation. Your induction year shouldn't really be seen as a series of hurdles to be feared. It can be an opportunity to reflect, consolidate and develop in a framework of support.

116

It is important to begin looking for a post early. Vacancies can come in fits and starts, and some posts are highly competitive, so it really does pay to start your job search early. Headteachers can advertise posts in a number of places:

o Internal LEA bulletins will be displayed in each school, so be sure to check them regularly for any vacancies.

o Agencies – these are not only used for the recruitment of supply or temporary teachers. There are a considerable number of agencies that deal solely or predominantly with teaching posts.

o Newspapers and magazines – the key publications to look out for here would probably be *The Times Educational Supplement* (*TES*), which comes out every Friday, and the *Guardian* on a Wednesday. Both carry a considerable number of job advertisements.

o Websites – again, there are a considerable number of websites that carry advertisements for teaching posts. Be sure that you check them frequently as they are generally updated daily. Many have a provision for you to be emailed any information regarding jobs that fit your criteria. The *TES* (www.tesjobs.co.uk) and *Guardian* (http://jobs.guardian.co.uk/education) websites, as well as those of LEAs aside, some good ones to check include: www.eteach.com; www.education-jobs.co.uk; www.jobsineducation.co.uk; www.theteachernet.co.uk; www.teachernet.gov.uk; www.hays.com/education; and www.teachers.eu.com.

o Contacts – in education, as in many other sectors, you may find out about jobs through contacts you have made – particularly if you want to teach in the same area in which you have trained. Cultivate your contacts, let people know that you are looking for work and ask them to inform you if anything comes up.

YOUR APPLICATION

Be sure to apply for posts as early as you can, and don't put off applying for other posts while you wait to hear if you will be called to interview. Before applying for a post, gather information. Send off for an application pack; look up the school's website and any Ofsted reports you may find; look to see if there are several vacancies in the same school; work out if you are right for the job and if the job is right for you and so on. Look carefully at the job description and underline key words. What experience are they looking for? What roles will you be expected to fill?

Many teaching posts require you to complete an application form. It is quite common for these to follow a county-wide proforma and so becoming familiar with the lay out and requirements of the form is time well spent. Unlike a covering letter, the application form can limit your responses rather, and it may be hard to capture your brilliance within its set parameters, so be sure to be concise and select those elements that present you in the very best light. Don't be tempted to send a CV and covering letter instead. Your application will generally be overlooked at first glance if you do this. A sloppily presented application form with grammatical or spelling errors will not be looked upon favourably. Be absolutely sure that you practice writing your answers several times before you commit them to your form. Ask someone to read through them to check for any slip ups. Be sure to follow any instructions. If you are asked to write in block capitals or black ink, do so. When applying for your first post, remember to focus on the experiences you have had during your training. Your paper round doesn't really need to be discussed!

Whatever form a job application might take – CV and letter or application form – there will undoubtedly be a section where you will be required to write about yourself. The academic qualifications and teaching experiences of many NQTs will be relatively similar, and so it is the personal statement that really distinguishes you from the pack and can make your application stand out or fall down flat. It is also the section that many people feel most uncomfortable writing.

Firstly, of course, re-read the advertisement and focus on any specifics mentioned. These can help you form the basis of much of your personal statement as you show how your personal qualities and interests match the job requirements. Don't be embarrassed about saying what you are good at and what you have achieved. Avoid bland platitudes – rather than simply state that you are reliable and a good team worker, offer some specific evidence. You need to show what you can do, while keeping the focus on skills or achievements that are related to the job. Highlight your teaching strengths and how you have engaged your pupils.

It is good to show that you have outside interests and hobbies, but you needn't give a hugely detailed account of your passion for archery, pigeon racing or Impressionist painting. You are applying for a job, not a pen pal. Also, don't invent skills or talents that you don't have. Your fictional prowess at lacrosse or playing the recorder may be called upon – if not at interview, then at a later date.

This part of the application form is where your writing skills most come into play and are under most scrutiny. Write in full sentences, not notes or bullet points, unless specified. Try to vary sentence starters – 'I am', 'I have', 'I like' becomes repetitive quickly and can make you sound rather uninteresting. If writing isn't a real strength of yours, ask someone to check your personal statement before you commit it to your form or letter. Try to sound enthusiastic – remember that the person reading your application could have slogged their way through hundreds before yours. Enthusiasm can be infectious. Finally, be sure to keep a copy of your personal statement, so that you can be prepared for potential interview questions.

ALL ABOUT YOU . . . THE PERSONAL STATEMENT

YOUR CURRICULUM VITAE

Some posts request that you apply using a CV. Remember that your CV should allow you to summarize your qualifications, experience and qualities *succinctly* and pertinently. The DfES is developing a CV format for teachers, but until that time, you will need to think carefully about presentation and content. You need to make your CV stand out among the many that a potential employer may receive. Preparation is key here. While you may have to fine-tune your CV for each post, most teaching jobs at entry level will require similar keys skills, qualifications and experience. Write down any sections you wish to include – education, skills, employment history and so on – and jot down anything else that you might wish to include. Decide upon those that are most applicable to the post for which you are applying and use these to form the basis of your CV. Read through the job and person specification closely and be sure to show how you fit them.

Make sure you structure your CV clearly and use a maximum of two pages. Try to avoid cramming too much information into too little space – be selective. Put your personal details at the top of the front page, remembering to include contact details. It is often a good idea to outline your education next, particularly if you have little relevant experience. When outlining your experience, organize it in terms of chronology or appropriateness. Describe your skills and experience in positive language. The most significant proportion of your relevant skills and experience will be based on your training and placement. Ask your tutor or mentor to check through your CV and to offer their honest advice.

Your interview for your teaching post may well be quite unlike any other you have attended. It is fairly usual for the interview process to last a full day and may include a tour of the school, an informal interview, a sample lesson, a presentation before the interviewing panel and a formal interview in front of senior staff and governors. This can all be quite daunting.

As with any interview, it pays to be prepared. Use the preparation you did (having read and taken on board Idea 10 'Getting Your Bearings') at the start of your placement as a guide. Read through the school prospectus and website and make some brief notes. Be informed, but not judgemental. If you can show that you know some specific information about the school it shows you are keen. Similarly, read through the advert very closely. Make notes as to how you fulfil the job criteria. Make sure that you are familiar with key terms, phrases and ideas – it helps you feel and appear professional.

If during the interview you are unsure about a question, ask if it could be repeated. This also gives you vital thinking time. Don't ramble or digress, but show your knowledge and understanding – this is your time to make an impression. While the official formal interview may have a designated time slot, you should consider yourself in interview mode from the moment you step into the school. Practise your answers with your tutor, mentor or a friend and find out what form the interview will take.

TOP TIPS FOR THE INTERVIEW

Interviews can be daunting. You are under pressure to impress within a set time. The following may help you feel and appear more confident.

o Dress smartly. This needn't mean wearing a suit, but you should look professional. Avoid any garish patterns or items which dominate your look. You want the attention to be on you, not your tights or tie. Try on your clothes well in advance of your interview date and check for missing buttons, fit and so on. Ensure that you are well groomed and neat.

o Check the route to the school in advance. Be sure to leave plenty of time to get there. Being late not only gives a bad impression, but it will leave you feeling nervous and unsettled.

o Take a portfolio with you of key documents and any examples of resources, pupils' work, assessment and so on. It will be useful to be able to call upon evidence of your achievements and this can help focus your attention before you go in.

o Be confident in your body language. Sit upright, but not stiff, with your feet on the floor. Avoid fidgeting with jewellery or clothes. Maintain eye contact – you are going to be interviewed by a panel, so be sure to include everyone.

o Use Standard English in your responses and make sure you answer the question asked. Try to give succinct examples to illustrate your points, without lapsing into pure anecdote. You may well be asked if you have any questions yourself. Be prepared for this, and be sure that you listen to reponses in turn.

If you are asked to teach a sample lesson, find out as much information as you can about the class and the aims as you can. You will need to know how long the session will be, what age group you will be teaching, how many pupils will be in the class, what topic you will be teaching and what the lesson aims are, what resources are available and so on. Remember that this is your chance to show what you can do, and well-considered resources and tasks can make a huge impact.

Make sure that you are ready. Produce any resources well in advance, ask your mentor or tutor to check them through and photocopy as many as you will need. If you are using PowerPoint or an IWB, ensure that the school system is available and compatible, and do have a backup plan. This is not the best time to try out a new technique or task – ensure that you feel comfortable in your choices, and that you show yourself in the best possible light. Find out what equipment will be available to you and try to use it.

Try to focus on your teaching *and* the pupils' learning – involve them in your lesson. Be enthusiastic and encouraging, and use praise. If a class-management issue arises (rare, but possible) it is not the end of the world. What is important is how you deal with any problems once they arise. It can sometimes be useful to refer to your lesson in the interview, maybe commenting on the choices you made and so on. Your lesson will often be quite short and so a structure that demonstrates your awareness of good practice is important. Try to include a short starter activity, introduce clear objectives for the lesson, a key task (or more if time allows) and a plenary and summing up.

Supply teachers make up a considerable part of the teaching workforce, covering anything from short notice, single-day absences to long-term maternity leave. The benefits of supply work include flexibility, freedom from inspections, meetings and paperwork but you can miss out on further training, the opportunity to develop effective relationships with pupils and colleagues, and so on. As a supply teacher, you are paid a flat daily rate and you will not be paid holiday or sick pay. It is worth noting that to be paid full teaching rate for your supply work you should be a member of the General Teaching Council.

As soon as you have passed your course and gained QTS, you are eligible for supply work. Contact your LEA and put yourself on their supply register. There are also many recruitment agencies that match teachers with schools. Be sure to check pay rates and conditions of service before signing up.

You will usually be able to work through part of your induction year on a supply basis if an appointment is for a term or longer, although this would usually have to be agreed with the school beforehand. It is more usual for term-length or longer contracts to be temporary, rather than supply. As a rule, NQTs can do casual supply work for four terms before they have to find a post in which they can embark on their induction programme.

A working day for a supply teacher should be 6.5 hours. This may, although rarely does in most short-term supply posts, include duties other than classroom teaching. As a supply teacher, you may well find yourself teaching subjects other than your own. You will certainly be teaching pupils you do not know. Remember that your job is to teach the class, not simply supervise them. Work will usually have been set by the class teacher and resources left for you to deliver, but this aside, you should treat supply lessons as you would any other. You are there as a member of the teaching staff and word – good or bad – spreads very quickly.

The lure of sunnier climes or different cultures can be very appealing. Once you have completed your training and are browsing through the pages of the *TES*, you may well find your eye drawn to jobs in other countries. These jobs will vary hugely, from small private language schools to international schools that follow the UK National Curriculum.

Before you set your heart on a teaching post in another country, it is worth considering a few things. In terms of induction, it is generally the case that you will be unable to commence your induction programme in another country. There are some exceptions to this such as British schools in Gibraltar, Guernsey, Jersey and the Isle of Man, as well as Service Children's schools in Germany and Cyprus. Even in these instances, it is still important to check that induction is available. There is, however, nothing to stop you from teaching overseas and then starting your induction programme upon your return. If you wish to teach in a British or international school, you may be wise to get some experience first, and certainly to get your induction year out of the way. Some such schools specify two years' experience as a matter of course.

Some agencies recruit teachers for posts overseas – such as VIF who recruit for the USA – and deal with visa applications, work permits and so on, but completion of induction is often a proviso.

Many overseas jobs do not specify any length of experience and welcome NQTs. But be careful. Reputable schools will usually expect an interview, even if only by phone, before employing you. Have a firm understanding of pay and accommodation before you leave, as well as contact addresses and numbers of the school employing you. Also, ensure that you understand any visa or other requirements of the country in which you will be working, as well as any cultural or social mores. Working in another country can be an incredible experience, just be sure that your expectations and preparation are realistic. There are numerous websites and books dedicated to teaching in another country. Do your homework before you commit yourself.

Useful Information

TEACHING UNIONS AND ORGANIZATIONS

There are a number of organizations that you can join as a trainee teacher. Many of them will offer membership free or at a reduced rate for trainee teachers. You may be asked to join unions, Teaching Councils, subject-specific organizations and so on. The following is by no means a comprehensive review, but offers you information regarding the most prominent organizations.

Membership of one of the General Teaching Councils, for England, Ireland, Scotland or Wales, is mandatory for all teachers – including those working part time or on supply contracts – in maintained schools. These are professional bodies, independent from government, with statutory, advisory and regulatory powers. As they are self-financing, much of their income comes from the yearly fees (currently £30) paid by teachers, although this is compensated for by way of tax relief. The GTC offers members, among other things, the opportunity to participate in national conferences and events, funding opportunities for professional development, and advice.

Union membership is elective, but strongly recommended. During your training, you will generally be offered membership for free. There are a number of teaching unions – the largest being the NUT, the NASUWT and the ATL – with sometimes very different ideals and structures. Shop around and decide which one is for you. Being a member of a union means that you have access to support – legal, if necessary – training, information, advice, as well as representation.

Teacher training is hard work. Not only do you have to cope with the day-to-day demands of classroom teaching and whole-school life, but you will have to commit yourself to academic study of your subject and teaching per se. If at all possible, it is very useful to get some reading under your belt *before* the course begins, as time really is at a premium then.

Familiarize yourself with the National Curriculum Orders for your subject; read the exam syllabuses of examination boards popular in your area and become a frequent visitor to key websites such as the Teacher Training Agency (www.tta.gov.uk); the Department for Education and Skills (www.dfes.gov.uk) and *The Times Educational Supplement* (www.tes.co.uk) and the websites of the various teaching unions – some others are listed in Idea 98.

Read through some of the many subject-specific teaching guides available – the ways in which you will use your subject knowledge in the classroom will be very different from the ways you were tested on it for your degree. Also, be sure to read some books which deal with teaching and education, such as *Getting the Buggers to Behave* by Sue Cowley, *Becoming a Teacher* edited by Justin Dillon or *Essential Teaching Skills* by Chris Kyriacou. Try to ensure that you read books that are relevant to the experiences you anticipate. A book about teaching in the 1940s will be interesting, and may well raise some issues, but also examine books that outline current themes, developments and strategies. Become familiar with key terms, concepts and debates, and visit websites regularly.

This list is by no means comprehensive nor an assertion of excellence in comparison to those not listed. I have tried to stay away from resource sites and give you the addresses of websites that can help you become familiar with concepts, skills, documentation and so on.

WEBSITES

www.teachernet.gov.uk
www.activecitizens.org.uk
www.risetrust.org.uk
www.aqa.org.uk
www.teachingcitizenship.org.uk
www.aaia.org.uk
www.byteachers.org.uk
www.bbc.co.uk/education
www.becta.org.uk
www.behaviour4learning.ac.uk
www.bda-dyslexia.org.uk
www.accac.org.uk
www.curriculumonline.gov.uk
www.dea.org.uk
www.estyn.gov.uk
www.gtce.org.uk; www.gtcni.org.uk; www.gtcs.org.uk
www.get.teachers.tv
www.kidscape.org.uk
www.learn.co.uk
www.learningwales.gov.uk
www.ncaction.org.uk
www.nc.uk.net
www.ngfl.gov.uk
www.qca.org.uk
www.senteacher.org
www.talkingteaching.co.uk
www.tre.ngfl.gov.uk
www.teachersupport.info
www.thegrid.org.uk

During the initial weeks of your training, there may be times when you feel as if you have stumbled into a kind of secret society with its own private language, and find yourself silently nodding as those around you speak in code. You will quickly become au fait with many of the most pertinent terms and abbreviations, but the following glossary, while by no means exhaustive, should help you feel a little more confident.

ACCAC – Awdurdod Cymwysterau Cwricwlwm ac Asesu Cymru: Qualifications Curriculum and Assessment Authority for Wales.

ADD – Attention Deficit Disorder.

ADHD – Attention Deficit Hyperactivity Disorder.

AQA – Assessment and Qualifications Alliance.

AT – Attainment Target. These identify the skills, knowledge and understanding pupils should have acquired by the end of each Key Stage. Attainment targets for the statutory subjects include graduated level descriptors.

ATL – Association of Teachers and Lecturers.

ASD – Autistic Spectrum Disorder.

AST – Advanced Skills Teacher.

ATL – Association of Teachers and Lecturers.

BA with QTS – Batchelor of Arts with Qualified Teacher Status.

BDA – British Dyslexia Association.

BECTA – British Educational Communications and Technology Agency. This is the key government agency for ICT in education.

BEd with QTS – Batchelor of Education with Qualified Teacher Status.

BTEC – Business and Technical Education Council. This body validates vocational courses including NVQs, GNVQs and Ordinary or Higher National Diplomas.

CAT – Cognitive Ability Test – often used by schools at the start of Year 7.

Catchment Area – Some schools give admissions priority to those pupils who live in a designated area around or near the school. This is known as the catchment area.

CEDP – Career Entry and Development Profile

GLOSSARY OF TERMS A–I

CED – Career Entry Profile

Community School – Schools wholly maintained and owned by the LEA.

CPI – Child Protection Issue.

CRAC – Careers Research and Advisory Centre.

DfES – Department for Education and Skills.

Dyspraxia – An impairment of the organization of movement caused by visual-motor and kinaesthetic-motor difficulites. Once known as 'clumsy child syndrome'.

EAL – English as an Additional Language.

EAZs – Education Action Zones.

EBD – Emotional and Behavioural Difficulties.

EDP – Education Development Plan.

ESL – English as a Second Language.

Estyn – The office of Her Majesty's Inspectorate in Wales.

EWO – Education Welfare Officer.

Feeder Schools – Primary schools, usually within a catchment area, which have priority for admission to a given secondary school.

Foundation School – State school, run by LEA, but with more freedoms regarding management and admissions.

FSM – Free School Meals.

GCSE – General Certificate of Secondary Education.

GNVQ – General National Vocational Qualification.

GTC – General Teaching Council.

Grant Maintained School – State schools that are funded centrally rather than via their LEA.

GTP – Graduate Teacher Programme.

GTTR – Graduate Teacher Training Registry.

HMI – Her Majesty's Inspector.

ICT – Information and Communication Technology

IEP – Individual Education Plan. Plan devised by the SENCO and class teacher to address the particular needs of and provide the specific support for those pupils.

ILP – Individual Learning Plan

INSET – In-service Education and Training.

ITT – Initial Teacher Training.

IWB – Interactive Whiteboard

Key Skills – These are skills extra to and underpinning post-16 study. They are Communications; Application of Number; Information Technology. Wider key skills units are also available. These are Working with Others; Improving Own Learning; Performance and Problem Solving.

KS – Key Stage. The NC is ordered into Key stages 1–4. Key Stage 1 generally covers school Years 1 and 2; Key Stage 2 – Years 3 to 6; Key Stage 3 – Years 7 to 9 and Key Stage 4 – Years 10 and 11.

LEA – Local Education Authority.

LSA – Learning Support Assistant.

Maintained Schools – Schools that are funded publicly.

MLD – Mild Learning Difficulties.

NASUWT – National Association of Schoolmasters and Union of Women Teachers.

NC – National Curriculum.

NFER – National Foundation for Educational Research.

NLP – National Literacy Project.

NLS – National Literacy Strategy.

NQT – Newly Qualified Teacher.

NRA – National Record of Achievement.

NUT – National Union of Teachers.

NVQ – National Vocational Qualification

Ofsted – Office for Standards in Education.

OHP – Overhead Projector.

OMR – Optical Mark Reader.

PEP – Personal Education Plan. These plans support the education of young people in care.

PGCE – Postgraduate Certificate of Education.

PMLD – Profound and Multiple Learning Difficulties.

PoS – Programme of Study. Each NC subject has a PoS that outlines what should be taught at each Key Stage.

PSE – Personal and Social Education.

PSHE – Personal, Social and Health Education.

PTA – Parent Teacher Association.

QCA – Qualifications and Curriculum Authority.

QTS – Qualified Teacher Status.

SAT – Standard Assessment Task/Test.

Scheme of Work – this is a document outlining how the PoS is to be covered in a given subject. Schemes of Work are usually broken into manageable sections, with activities and resources.

SEN – Special Educational Needs. Learning difficulty or gifted.

SENCO – Special Educational Needs Coordinator.

SLD – Severe Learning Difficulties.

SMT – Senior Management Team.

SpLD – Specific Learning Difficulty.

Statement – Statements describe any particular needs the named pupil has and specifies the assistance and support they will require.

TA – Teacher Assessment.

TA – Teaching Assistant.

TES – Times Educational Supplement.

Transition – This is used to denote movement between Key Stages, as well as between phases of a lesson.

TTA – Teacher Training Agency.

Value added – This looks at the achievements of pupils in comparison with their attainment level and potential at point of intake, rather than simply using final grade achieved as an indicator of accomplishment. Thus, the degree of progress made in a school as opposed to grades alone is the focus of a value-added approach.

VIF – Visiting International Faculty Program.